IMAGES
*of America*

# SEATTLE'S MAYFLOWER PARK HOTEL

Hooked on History...!
enjoy the read!
Trish Festa

Sharing the love of
Mayflower history...
one story at a
time.

Enjoy!

[signature]

# PROCLAMATION

WHEREAS, the city of Seattle recognizes and appreciates the many businesses and organizations that help drive our economy and community toward success; and

WHEREAS, the Mayflower Park Hotel on Fourth and Olive in downtown Seattle is one of the last remaining historic hotels in continuous operation since 1927; and

WHEREAS, as a locally owned and operated establishment, the Mayflower Park Hotel ensures that visitors from all over the world who work in and visit our city receive a sincere Northwest greeting and feel comfortable; and

WHEREAS, on July 16, 2007, friends and family of the Mayflower Park Hotel will celebrate the hotel's 80th anniversary and reflect on eight decades of outstanding service and hospitality;

NOW, THEREFORE, I, GREGORY J. NICKELS, Mayor of the city of Seattle, do hereby proclaim July 16, 2007 to be

## MAYFLOWER PARK HOTEL DAY

in Seattle, and I encourage the community to join me in recognizing this outstanding local business for eighty years of success.

GREG NICKELS
Mayor

MAYFLOWER PARK HOTEL DAY. This proclamation by the City of Seattle, issued by Mayor Greg Nickels, proclaimed July 16, 2007, to be Mayflower Park Hotel Day in recognition of the hotel's 80th anniversary.

ON THE COVER: THE NEIGHBORHOOD IN 1939. The hotel was part of a vibrant city scene in 1939. Hotel Mayflower's rooftop neon sign and the four-story neon sign on the northwest corner of the building reflected the trend of that era when colorful neon signs dominated the city streets of Seattle. See page 44 for this street scene at night. (Courtesy of Seattle Municipal Archives 38853.)

IMAGES
*of America*

# SEATTLE'S MAYFLOWER PARK HOTEL

Trish Festin, Audrey McCombs,
Craig Packer, and Stevie Festin

ARCADIA
PUBLISHING

Published by Arcadia Publishing
Charleston, South Carolina

Printed in the United States of America

Library of Congress Control Number: 2013947614

For all general information, please contact Arcadia Publishing:
Telephone 843-853-2070
Fax 843-853-0044
E-mail sales@arcadiapublishing.com
For customer service and orders:
Toll-Free 1-888-313-2665

Visit us on the Internet at www.arcadiapublishing.com

*This book is dedicated to Birney and Marie Dempcy for their steadfast dedication as caretakers of the Mayflower Park Hotel; to the wonderful staff, who exemplify genuine and authentic hospitality; and to our loyal guests, who have returned to us time and time again. Together our story is "Quite Simply, One of a Kind."*

# CONTENTS

# ACKNOWLEDGMENTS

The Mayflower Park Hotel Historical Society members would like to thank the many people who helped make this book possible.

Thank you, Birney and Marie Dempcy, for your blessing on this project. Your hard work as well as dedication to every detail is an inspiration. The story needed to be told and it is an honor you allowed us to tell it.

Thank you, Stacia Williams, director of marketing and communications at the Mayflower Park Hotel, for your editing knowledge and thoughtful feedback, which were integral to this book.

Thank you, Paul Ishii, general manager at the Mayflower Park Hotel, and our colleagues and our families for your support and enthusiasm, which encouraged us along the way.

Thank you, Cheryl Gunselman and Pat Mueller, at Manuscripts, Archives, and Special Collections, Washington State University Libraries. Pat joined in on our excitement in 2006 when we discovered the motherlode of Mayflower historical information in the archives at Washington State University Libraries. Cheryl provided the professional guidance and support we needed to credit information properly.

Thank you, Dr. Lorraine McConaghy, at the Museum of History & Industry. Lorraine has always been our go-to person on anything historical. Lorraine gave our project credibility by endorsing our proposal to Arcadia Publishing and gave us assistance in finding images we needed for this book.

Thank you, University of Washington, Special Collections, and the Seattle Public Library for your collections of periodicals and digital images.

Thank you, Gonzaga University, for providing an internship program for history majors. We were honored to have Stevie Festin, a member of Phi Alpha Theta National History Honor Society, as a valuable partner on this book.

A thank-you goes to all the guests, employees, and people of Seattle for sharing your Mayflower Park Hotel memories. Those stories gave our history life. Keep them coming!

History has always been something that has set the Mayflower Park Hotel apart from most Seattle hotels. We have it, and we embrace it. When the hotel celebrated its 80th anniversary, we decided to dig deep and find out more about our history. The more we uncovered, the more excited we became. So we dug and dug and dug. Five years later, we had filled 12 binders of historical information.

Armed with these binders, we submitted a proposal to Arcadia Publishing. Our proposal was accepted, and thus, the publishing journey began.

We had no idea about the magnitude of this project. The guidelines and deadlines from Arcadia Publishing were challenging. However, looking back, it was those guidelines and deadlines that motivated us to publish our story. Thank you, Rebecca Coffey, for your patience with ordinary hotel people who love the Mayflower Park Hotel. Any errors or omissions are strictly unintentional.

Unless otherwise noted, all images appear courtesy of the Mayflower Park Hotel and all text taken from the Mayflower Park Hotel website is used with the permission of the hotel.

# Letter from the Owners

We are very excited to showcase the history of the Mayflower Park Hotel. Built in 1927 by local owners, it was one of Seattle's finest hotels, and now 87 years later, it is still locally owned and is still an important part of our community.

When we bought the hotel in 1973, it was not our intention to become as totally involved as we did. The hotel had been neglected and was in bad repair. But as the renovation of the building progressed, we, as so many others, fell in love with its emerging charm and became dedicated to its restoration.

Along the way, we were fortunate to work with wonderful employees, architects, designers, and others who shared our vision and contributed ideas, dedication, and loyalty. They are all part of the Mayflower Park Hotel's family, and to them, we offer our profound thanks. Also, much gratitude must be expressed to our partners for their incredible and unwavering support over the years.

Most importantly, a hotel is about people. Over the years, the Mayflower Park Hotel has been privileged to be a participant in the major and minor events of people's lives—mostly happy, occasionally sad, but always important to those involved. To our guests, many of whom have returned to us time and time again, we are deeply indebted.

For us, it has been a privilege to be caretakers of this lovely and very special hotel for the past 40 years. These years have brought us much satisfaction and joy, and we are dedicated to the tradition of making the Mayflower Park Hotel "Quite Simply, One of a Kind."

—Birney and Marie Dempcy

*An Entrance to Hospitality*

"AN ENTRANCE TO HOSPITALITY." A 1934 brochure described the Hotel Mayflower, "One of Seattle's newest hotels with twelve stories of modern fireproof construction—250 rooms all outside and all with private baths. The lounge and mezzanine were unusually beautiful. The hotel is in the very center of the smart uptown shopping and theater districts. It is within a block of the city's largest department stores, and across the street from the Orpheum and famous Seattle Public Market. The Banquet Rooms accommodate 10–250 guests, with rates based on menu desired." (Courtesy of Museum of History & Industry, PEMCO Webster & Stevens Collection.)

# One

# BERGONIAN HOTEL
## 1927–1933

The Mayflower Park Hotel started its life as the Bergonian Hotel on July 16, 1927, and has been in continuous operation ever since. Opening festivities included an orchestra concert as well as a swaying throng of dancers who glided over the checkered mosaic ballroom floor until midnight.

One of Seattle's first "uptown" hotels, it was designed by architect B. Dudley Stuart, took six months to build, and cost $750,000. The name "Bergonian" came from the owner Stephen Berg and his love of the newspaper the *Oregonian* out of Portland, Oregon. Berg was a prominent builder of the time who obtained the first building permit of the year in 1927. He personally chose furnishings that were the best obtainable. The hotel had 240 rooms and according to the *Seattle Daily Times* of July 15, 1927, they were "all with baths." Opening prices for rooms ranged from $2 to $3.50 for one person and $3 to $4.50 for two persons. Rooms with twin beds were more expensive at $4 to $5.50, and suites ranged from $5 to $10. The lobby was decorated with deeply napped oriental carpets, palm trees, mirrors, brass, iron fixtures, and a fountain filled with goldfish in the center. The barbershop and the Bergonian Coffee Shop could be entered from Olive Way. Prices in the coffee shop, which seated 54, ranged from 20¢ for a cup of chicken broth to $2 for a sirloin steak for two. Coffee was 10¢. The beauty parlor was located off the Ladies' Lounge on the mezzanine. The cigar stand, with its handsome walnut cabinets, was located opposite the elevators.

The 1929 stock market crash had a devastating effect on Seattle and the entire United States, and Stephen Berg was not spared. He declared bankruptcy and lost everything. Silverstone Brothers, the landowner, became the hotel operator during the foreclosure process, maintaining the Bergonian Hotel's reputation as a leading Seattle hotel.

**THE NEIGHBORHOOD IN 1909.** During the 1880s, Seattle was racing toward new status as a major metropolis. Beginning in 1903 and again in 1910, Denny Hill, which covered 62 city blocks, was whittled away by continuous blasts of water and became known as the Denny Regrade. (Courtesy of University of Washington Libraries, Special Collections LEE040.)

**THE NEIGHBORHOOD IN 1916.** A panoramic view looking east toward Capitol Hill shows the Times Square Building under construction. The Waverly Apartments, across Olive Way to the south of the Times Square Building, occupies the site of the future Mayflower Park Hotel. (Courtesy of Museum of History & Industry, PEMCO Webster & Stevens Collection.)

**STEPHEN BERG.** Prior to building the Bergonian Hotel, Stephen Berg was one of the most prominent builders in Seattle. Other hotels he built and operated included the Continental Hotel, the Claremont Apartment-Hotel, and the Biltmore Apartments. He built over 600 single-family homes and was the first in Seattle to build one entire block of homes. (Courtesy of the Berg family.)

**BERGONIAN HOTEL UNDER CONSTRUCTION IN 1927.** Built by Stephen Berg, the Bergonian Hotel was the first building permit issued in 1927 by the City of Seattle. Architects were George Willington Stoddard, Bertram Dudley Stuart Jr., and Arthur Wheatley. Berg employed over 400 carpenters. (Courtesy of University of Washington Libraries, Special Collections Division UW27541.)

11

**BERGONIAN OPENS, JULY 16, 1927.**
Allan R. Thompson, opening manager,
was quoted in the *Seattle Daily
Times* on July 17, 1927, as saying, "In
selecting our staff we had in mind
only one consideration and that was
high-class service. It is our purpose
to make the Bergonian service of just
as high a character as the splendid
building." (Courtesy of University
of Washington Libraries, Special
Collections Division UW 26841.)

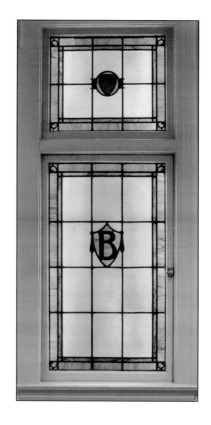

**STAINED-GLASS WINDOW.** This stained-glass
window, located on the mezzanine, has the letter
B for Bergonian. Eight stained-glass windows
were located on the mezzanine level.

**BERGONIAN HOTEL LOBBY.** *Seattle Daily Times* on July 17, 1927, reported, "With all the appointments of modern luxury—deeply napped Oriental carpets, fountains filled with playing goldfish, chandeliers like those of the Trianon, and numerous beautiful fixtures—the new Bergonian Hotel at Olive Street and Fourth Avenue opened its doors to the public at 6:30 p.m. last evening." (Courtesy of University of Washington Libraries, Special Collections Division UW26842.)

**PHIL COOK'S BARBERSHOP.** The barbershop's lobby entrance was located to the left of the stairs leading to the mezzanine. A customer of Phil Cook wrote, "Phil gave me a very good haircut and he talked about people having dirty necks. The next haircut he mentioned it again. That did it; it was time for a new barber." (Courtesy of University of Washington Libraries, Special Collections Division UW26224.)

**BERGONIAN HOTEL LADIES' LOUNGE.** Described as a quiet place for the ladies, the Ladies' Lounge was located on the mezzanine. Adjacent to it was the Bergonian Beauty Salon with windows that overlooked Olive Way. Records show the beauty salon was in business beginning in 1927 with the last mention of it in 1938. A customer in the 1930s wrote, "I had my first Permanent Wave at the Bergonian Hotel Beauty Salon. The first Permanent Wave machines were cumbersome and hot. They had a circle of curlers overhead and it took a long time to be wired onto them. Mrs. Galbraith referred to the process as enduring 'Pride Pains.' The results were beautiful for the style of the day. I had many permanents at the Bergonian Beauty Parlor, and fondly remember the Bergonian Hotel." (Courtesy of University of Washington Libraries, Special Collections Division UW27542.)

**BERGONIAN ENVELOPE WITH BEAUTY SHOP RETURN ADDRESS AND BERGONIAN POSTCARD.** These two pieces of hotel stationery show the exterior of the hotel from Fourth Avenue and Olive Way. Included in both scenes are pedestrians and cars as well as the Bergonian Hotel's two entrances, with the primary being on Olive Way and the secondary on Fourth Avenue. Just inside the Fourth Avenue entrance was the Where-To-Go Bureau. *Hotel News of the West* reported on June 14, 1930, "The Where-To-Go Bureau desk will handle all tourist and travel inquiries, arrange sightseeing trips for visitors, direct them to places of interest and give them information." (Courtesy of Craig Packer.)

BERGONIAN HOTEL, SEATTLE, WASH.

## COCKTAILS, RELISHES, APPETIZERS

| | | | | | |
|---|---|---|---|---|---|
| Crab Flake Cocktail | .35 | Ripe Olives | .20 | Anchovies in Oil | .50 |
| Merry Widow | .45 | Queen Olives | .25 | Anchovies on Tomatoes | .50 |
| Olympia Oyster | .35 | Radishes | .15 | Bergonian Appetizer | .75 |
| Puget Sound | .45 | Young Onions | .15 | Crab Meat Louis | .85 |
| Grapefruit | .30 | Pickled Onions | .25 | Chow Chow | .25 |
| Fruit | .25 | Major Grey Chutney | .25 | Caviar on Ice | 1.00 |
| Shrimp | .30 | Celery Hearts | .20 | Caviar Canape | .60 |
| Salted Almonds | .25 | Dill Pickles | .15 | Canape Modern | .75 |
| Stuffed Tomato Surprise | .40 | Sweet Pickles | .15 | Pickled Walnuts | .25 |

## OYSTERS

### OLYMPIA

| | | | |
|---|---|---|---|
| Raw on Plate | .60 | | |
| Stewed in Milk | .60 | | |
| Stewed in Cream | .70 | | |
| Pan Roast | .65 | | |
| Fancy Pepper Pan Roast | .75 | | |
| Fried | .70 | | |
| Scallops | .70 | | |
| Poulette | .90 | | |

### EASTERN

| | |
|---|---|
| Raw | .50 |
| Stewed in Cream | .75 |
| Stewed in Milk | .60 |
| Fried and Cold Slaw | .60 |
| Baked, With Bacon | .60 |
| Baked Kirkpatrick | .75 |
| Newburg | 1.00 |
| Bergonian Fried | .80 |

## SOUPS

| | | | |
|---|---|---|---|
| Consomme in Cup | .20 | Onion Soup au Gratin | .35 |
| Consomme in Cup with Eggs | .25 | Clam Chowder | .25 |
| Chicken Broth, Cup | .20 | Clam Broth | .20 |
| Puree Tomato Soup, Rice | .20 | Clear Green Turtle Soup | .35 |
| Cream of Tomato | .25 | Vegetable | .25 |

## FISH AND SHELLFISH

| | | | |
|---|---|---|---|
| Salmon Steak Maitre d'Hotel | .60 | Cracked Crabs Mayonnaise | .75 |
| Halibut Steak | .60 | Crab Meat Newburg | 1.00 |
| Fried Filet Sole, Tartar Sauce | .60 | Crab Meat au Gratin | .90 |
| Baked Filet Sole Mornay | .75 | Sand Dabs Meuniere | .60 |
| Fried Smelts Sauce Ravigotte | .50 | Salt Mackerel, Steamed Potatoes | .50 |
| Salmon Trout Meuniere | .70 | Finnan Haddie, Drawn Butter | .60 |

## STEAKS, CHOPS, CUTLETS, POULTRY

| | | | |
|---|---|---|---|
| Sirloin Steak for one | 1.00 | Top Sirloin Steak | .60 |
| Sirloin Steak for 2 | 2.00 | Pounded Steak with Onions | .75 |
| Tenderloin Steak, 1 | 1.00 | Pork Chops Plain | .60 |
| Tenderloin Steak, 2 | 2.00 | Pork Chops Breaded, Fried Apples | .80 |
| Steak a la Minute | .90 | Pork Tenderloin, Country Gravy | .75 |
| Lamb Chops (2) 50, (3) | .75 | Ham Steak Cooked in Honey Southern Style | 1.00 |
| Veal Cutlets Plain | .65 | Club Steak en Casserole | 1.00 |
| Veal Cutlets, Breaded, Tomato Sauce | .75 | Roast Beef Hash, Green Peppers | .50 |
| Weiners Schnitzel | .80 | Corned Beef Hash, Poached Egg | .50 |
| Mutton Chops (2) | .60 | Minced Chicken in Cream on Toast | .50 |
| Bergonian Grill | 1.00 | Lamb's Kidney, Bacon | .60 |
| Lamb Hash, Poached Egg | .60 | Fried Ham or Bacon | .50 |
| Ham and Eggs | .50 | Half Fried or Broiled Spring Chicken | 1.00 |
| Bacon and Eggs | .50 | Half Spring Chicken Paprika Sauce | 1.00 |
| Calf's Liver and Bacon | .60 | Chicken Flackes a la King | 1.00 |
| Hamburger Steak and Onions | .60 | Breast of Chicken under Glass a la | |
| Chicken Liver Saute on Toast | .60 | Bergonian | 1.50 |
| Lamb Kidney and Bacon | .60 | | |

Spring Chicken Maryland, Half 1.00, Whole 1.85

## GARNITURES

| | | | | | |
|---|---|---|---|---|---|
| Mushrooms Sauce | .35 | Rasher of Bacon (3 pieces) | .25 | Hollandaise Sauce | .40 |
| Spanish Sauce | .25 | Smothered Onions | .25 | Bearnaise Sauce | .40 |
| a la Stanley | .30 | Thousand Island | .15 | Bordelaise Sauce | .30 |

*Our chef will be pleased to prepare any special dish desired but which is not listed on this menu.*

*Banquets and Private Parties given special attention.*

*Reservations given in advance to the Head waiter will receive careful attention*

ROOM SERVICE  *For Orders in Room, A. M. 15c, P. M. 25c*

**BERGONIAN HOTEL COFFEE SHOP.** *Hotel News of the West* on July 16, 1927, reported, "The Coffee Shop seats 54 people. All fixtures are done in a walnut finish and waitresses are to wear silver gray aprons with coral collars and cuffs—a pleasing combination." On July 6, 1929, the publication reported, "It's not often that the large hotel of today finds the proprietor out bagging his own game or catching his own fish to be served in the dining room. Fish caught by Stephen Berg, proprietor of the Bergonian in Seattle, as a feature upon last Monday's menu offered as a novelty, proved to be a decided hit. Mr. Berg took his yacht to Possession Point and caught so many salmon that about 65 pounds of the fish were turned over to Chef Jake Dawn of the Bergonian. Guests seemed to enjoy the fresh fish caught by 'mine host' for the 75¢ per person dinner."

**PANORAMIC VIEW OF BERGONIAN HOTEL WITH PUGET SOUND IN THE BACKGROUND.** "Hotel Bergonian" is seen painted on the east side. Also pictured is the unique intersection of Fifth Avenue, Olive Way, and Stewart Street. Members of the Denny Party, most having arrived at Alki Beach in West Seattle on November 13, 1851, founded Seattle. William N. Bell; his wife, Sarah Bell; and their daughters Laura, Olive, Virginia, and Lavinia were included in the Denny Party. The neighborhood in which the hotel is located is often referred to as "Belltown." Seattle, King County, and State of Washington records legally describe the land on which the Hotel Bergonian sits as "Heirs of Sarah A. Bell." Olive Way was named after William and Sarah's second child Olive, and Stewart Street was named after Olive's husband, Joseph H. Stewart. (Courtesy of Museum of History & Industry.)

**GRAND OPENING ADVERTISEMENT OF BARTELL DRUGS NO. 13 AT THE BERGONIAN HOTEL.** Bartell Drugs was located in the Bergonian Hotel at the northwest corner as a street-level storefront. Note the items included in this advertisement "in celebration of the opening of store No. 13—Bergonian Hotel Fourth & Olive." When 21-year-old George H. Bartell Sr. founded Bartell Drugs in Seattle in 1890, he had a simple, clear vision to build a drugstore chain based on better customer service and top value. Over 100 years later, there are 58 stores in the Puget Sound region. (Courtesy of Bartell Drugs.)

**BARTELL DRUGS NO. 13.** This is a street view of the Bergonian Hotel. Located in the Bergonian Hotel storefront at the corner of Fourth Avenue and Olive Way, Bartell Drugs No. 13 opened on July 19, 1928. The store contained a small soda fountain and operated at this location until 1946. Five elaborate store display windows advertised products for sale such as "Jumbo Hot Ovaltine or Hot Chocolate" for 15¢. Bartell Drugs recycles its store numbers, and store No. 13 is now located in Bellevue, Washington. (Above, courtesy of Museum of History & Industry, PEMCO Webster & Stevens Collection; below, courtesy of Bartell Drugs.)

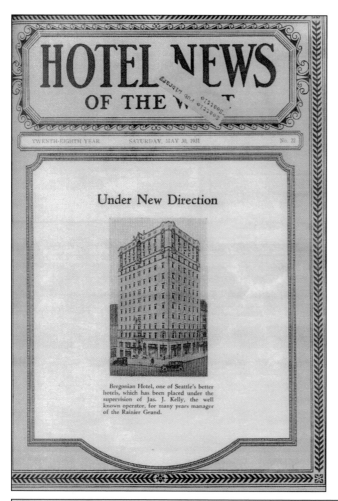

**Under New Direction**

Bergonian Hotel, one of Seattle's better hotels, which has been placed under the supervision of Jas. J. Kelly, the well known operator, for many years manager of the Rainier Grand.

HOTEL NEWS OF THE WEST FRONT-PAGE STORY, "UNDER NEW DIRECTION." Seaboard Securities took ownership and active involvement in operational management of the Bergonian Hotel. *Hotel News of the West* reported on November 28, 1931, "No immediate changes in the hotel are contemplated, and the staff remains the same." After a few months of operational management, Seaboard Securities hired R.P. Ward, a well-known Seattle hotel man, to manage. *Hotel News of the West* reported on December 5, 1931, "Mr. Ward is replacing paint with paper upon the walls of a number of rooms. This change will be made gradually throughout the hotel, having found that guests prefer the 'homey' atmosphere which good wall paper gives." (Left, courtesy of Seattle Public Library; below, courtesy of Patricia Walker.)

ELiot 8700

**BERGONIAN HOTEL**

R. P. WARD,
Manager

Fourth at Olive
SEATTLE, WASH.

**HOTEL NEWS OF THE WEST FRONT-PAGE STORY, "THE BERGONIAN STEPS FORWARD."** The *Seattle Daily Times* reported on March 8, 1933, "With beautiful decorative effects and many novel features, including an old fashioned well, Seattle's newest dining place, the Jack and Jill Grill, opens today to the public in the Bergonian Hotel. The cheerfully painted walls depicting scenes of the popular Mother Goose rhyme of Jack and Jill lend the place a lively atmosphere. They were painted by Franz Zallinger of the distinguished Puget Sound Artist Group." *Hotel News of the West* reported on March 11, 1933, "More than 1,200 persons attended the invitational preview inspection of the new Jack and Jill Grill and Terrace Dining Room at the Seattle Bergonian Hotel Tuesday afternoon and evening. Mrs. Sybal Hamrick, Business Manager of Seattle's newest fine catering establishment said yesterday. . . . Wednesday the premises were crowded all day with patrons making the formal opening day a long-to-be remembered event for the enthusiastic management, staff and patrons of the Grill and Dining Room." (Courtesy of Seattle Public Library.)

**Jack and Jill Grill at the Bergonian Hotel.** Jack and Jill Grill operated at the Bergonian from March 8, 1933 to November 30, 1933. *Hotel News of the West* reported on March 4, 1933, "The Jack and Jill Grill shows the magic touch of the artist's brush . . . These are the handiworks of Franz Zallinger, Austrian artist, under the direction of A.F. Shepard Company, Seattle decorators." (Courtesy of Museum of History & Industry, PEMCO Webster & Stevens Collection.)

**The Great Seattle Fire Mural.** This mural was unveiled at the Museum of History & Industry. Franz Zallinger, the artist who painted the murals in the Jack and Jill Grill, had a son, Rudolph, who also was a talented artist. In 1953, Rudolph Zallinger was commissioned by General Insurance Company of America, today's SAFECO, to research and paint the great Seattle fire of 1889. The mural was unveiled in 1956 at the Museum of History & Industry, where it remains today. (Courtesy of Museum of History & Industry.)

# *Two*

# TO BE THE MAYFLOWER
# 1933–1973

During the Great Depression the hotel became one of the first properties managed by Western Hotels Inc. in the Northwest. On November 19, 1933, the *Seattle Daily Times* reported, "The chief significance of this transaction is that it is the first instance of a large piece of property which has been foreclosed being redeemed since the depression." On December 1, 1933, the hotel's name was changed to Hotel Mayflower, and it rapidly underwent a transformation in which the lobby was completely redecorated. Renovations continued with the installation of a rooftop neon sign with huge red letters measuring eight feet high with an overall dimension of 52 by 32 feet. It is believed to be one of the first neon signs in Seattle and one of the largest to be installed on a roof at that time.

In the ensuing years the Hotel Mayflower had various owners; the most prominent was Western Hotels Inc., now recognized as Westin Hotel and Resorts. In those early days, the Hotel Mayflower was a stepping-stone for many hotel managers who would eventually hold leadership roles with Westin. The most prominent was J. William Keithan, the Westin vice president who conceived, collected, and organized the Westin Archives, now located at Washington State University.

The Hotel Mayflower was sold to the Doric Company in 1955 and the name was changed to Mayflower Hotel. That same year the Doric Company, according to the *Pacific Northwest Hotel News* of August 1956, "acquired the New Washington, Mar Monte, The Leamington and The Black Angus." The company grew to a chain of 22 hotels, and Floyd Clodfelter was the "guiding genius and sparkplug behind the company's success." The Doric Company became the "new star in the hotel scene." In 1961, Floyd Clodfelter asked his brother Warren Clodfelter, of the Clodfelter and Bowden law firm, to guide him in selling the company. Warren gave this assignment to a young attorney he had just hired, Birney Dempcy. This assignment included working with Gene Autry, the Hollywood western movie star, and his associates who were interested in purchasing the hotels. He ended up buying only two hotels, which did not include the Mayflower. The Seattle downtown began to decline as residences and businesses moved to the suburbs. In 1964, the Doric Company faded into reorganization, resulting in a decade of decline for the Mayflower Hotel.

# HOTEL NEWS OF THE WEST

30TH YEAR    FRIDAY, DECEMBER 1, 1933    Number 29

## To Be The Mayflower

▲

The Hotel Bergonian, Seattle, which has been taken over by a new operating company, and will be re-named the Mayflower. An extensive improvement program has also been announced

▼

**"TO BE THE MAYFLOWER."** *Hotel News of the West* reported on December 1, 1933, "The Bergonian was built by Stephen Berg who operated it for several years with outstanding success. One of Seattle's leading commercial hotels, it was one of the victims of the depression however, and Mr. Berg was finally obliged to relinquish it to the mortgage holders who operated it for two years. Fourth and Olive Corporation redeemed the property. . . . Approximately $25,000 will be expended immediately for improvements which include a complete redecorating program, new carpets and new furnishings. The hotel will be renamed the Mayflower." (Courtesy of Seattle Public Library.)

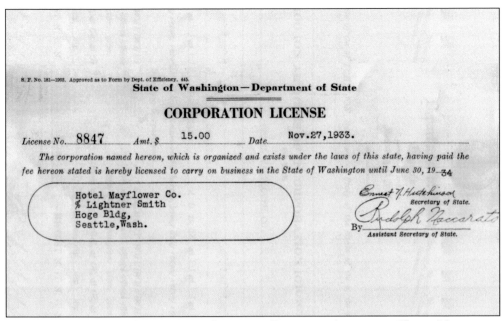

S. F. No. 181—1983. Approved as to Form by Dept. of Efficiency. 445.

### State of Washington—Department of State

## CORPORATION LICENSE

License No. **8847**    Amt. $ **15.00**    Date **Nov.27,1933.**

*The corporation named hereon, which is organized and exists under the laws of this state, having paid the fee hereon stated is hereby licensed to carry on business in the State of Washington until June 30, 19*__34__

> Hotel Mayflower Co.
> % Lightner Smith
> Hoge Bldg,
> Seattle,Wash.

*Ernest N. Hutchinson*
Secretary of State.

*Rudolph Naccarato*
By _____
Assistant Secretary of State.

**DEPARTMENT OF STATE, OFFICE OF THE SECRETARY FILING FOR ARTICLES OF HOTEL MAYFLOWER RECEIPT AND HOTEL MAYFLOWER SEAL.** The cost was $15 to file articles for the Hotel Mayflower Company on November 27, 1933. A special meeting of the board of trustees for Maltby-Thurston Hotels Inc. was held on October 30, 1933, to discuss the redemption. . . . The board authorized a joint redemption by Fourth & Olive Inc., the holder of the redemption right, and a corporation to be formed by Maltby-Thurston. These documents represent the results of that special meeting. (Both, courtesy of Manuscripts, Archives, and Special Collections, Washington State University Libraries.)

**SHAREHOLDER CERTIFICATE FOR HOTEL MAYFLOWER COMPANY.** One of the original shareholders was Edmond J. Meany, who owned one share of stock represented by this certificate, which was dated January 22, 1934. Meany was one of the University of Washington's most notable history professors. The bylaws of the Hotel Mayflower Company indicate that the share cost in January 1934 was $3.15, and the articles of incorporation authorized a total of 7,940 shares. The transfer agent and registrar was the Seattle Trust Company, which was authorized to execute and deliver all documents necessary to carry out the purposes of issuance and transfer of stock. The Seattle Trust Company was authorized to apply the proceeds of the stock sale to the principal and interest of a loan in the sum of $10,000. (Courtesy of Manuscripts, Archives, and Special Collections, Washington State University Libraries.)

**1933 NEWSPAPER ADVERTISEMENT FOR THE HOTEL MAYFLOWER AND 1933 POSTCARD.**
The postcard highlights the places that surround the Hotel Mayflower: Mount Rainier; Snoqualmie Falls; Grouse Mountain Chalet, Vancouver, British Columbia; Butchart's Garden, Victoria, British Columbia; Mount Baker; Seattle skyline; South Elliott Bay; motor ferry *Kalakala*, world's first steamline vessel; Civic Auditorium; and US government locks, the world's second largest locks. The back of the postcard boasts, "Seattle—The Gateway to the Olympic Peninsula. One of the World's greatest recreational areas; One of Seattle's newest and finest hotels; Unexcelled location; 12 Floors; Excellent combination coffee shop and dining room; service features of travel information desk, public stenographer, beauty parlor, barbershop, cigar stand, news service and drugstore; rates from $2 per day." (Right, courtesy of Seattle Public Library.)

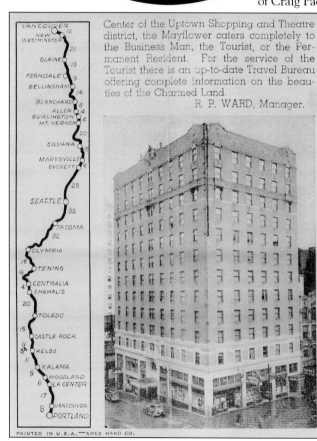

**1933 HOTEL MAYFLOWER LUGGAGE STICKER.** The slogan "The Charm of Yesterday— The Convenience of Today" was used despite the fact the hotel had only been in operation for five years. It was common for other Mayflower-named hotels across the country to use an image of the *Mayflower* in their logos. (Courtesy of Craig Packer.)

**1933 HOTEL BROCHURE.** *Hotel News of the West* reported in May 1934, "The Mayflower, Seattle has just issued an attractive new folder, showing pictorial attractions of the newly finished hotel. The pamphlet is done in a combination orange and silver, with clear half-tone illustrations." (Courtesy of Craig Packer.)

**HOTEL MAYFLOWER LOBBY IN 1934.** *Hotel News of the West* reported in February 1934, "The lobby has been completely rearranged, redecorated, and will be re-carpeted and refurnished soon. The front office desk has been moved opposite the elevators, where the cigar stand was, which has been moved to the opposite side of the entrance. The Fourth Avenue entrance has been closed and will be used as a small storeroom." (Courtesy of Museum of History & Industry, PEMCO Webster & Stevens Collection.)

**HOTEL MAYFLOWER MEZZANINE IN 1934.** A Mayflower guest shared the following, "In 1937, my piano teacher, Miss Persis Horton announced to her students that a recital would take place at the Hotel Mayflower in two weeks. All of the families were so excited to be attending a performance in this grand setting that we had all arrived early! The music was very important, but playing in one of the great hotels of Seattle was a young girl's dream. A young girl turned into a young lady that night—and it all happened at the Hotel Mayflower!" (Courtesy of Museum of History & Industry, PEMCO Webster & Stevens Collection.)

Seattle, Washington

# TARIFF BULLETIN

OF THE

# HOTEL MAYFLOWER

SEASON, 1934

## ACCOMMODATIONS

## and

## LOCATION

One of Seattle's newest Modern Hotels. 12 stories of modern fireproof construction — 250 rooms all outside and all with private Bath. Unusually beautiful Lounge and Mezzanine.

The very center of the smart uptown Shopping and Theatre district. Within a block of the city's largest Department Stores, and across the street from the Orpheum and famous Seattle Public Market, FOURTH AVENUE AT OLIVE WAY.

## RESERVATIONS

## and RATES

Reservations should be made in advance in the usual way and will be given prompt and careful attention.

Please state names of guests and means and time of arrival,—also probable duration of stay and accommodations required.

| | |
|---|---|
| 1 Person | $2 to $3.50 |
| 2 Persons | $3 to $4.50 |
| Twin Beds | $4.00 to $5.50 |
| Suites | $5 to $10 |

10% Commission to Tour Agents on Room accounts only.

---

TO TRAVEL BUREAUS *and* AGENCIES........ We wish to co-operate with you in every way possible and if there is any further information you require you may wire at our expense. Descriptive folders on request.
R. P. WARD, *Manager.*

---

## COFFEE SHOP—BANQUET ROOMS

Every phase of the smart modern Coffee Shop is in charge of expert Dietitians.

| | |
|---|---|
| Luncheons from | 35c |
| Dinners from | 50c |
| Club Breakfasts from | 20c |

Banquet Rooms with accommodation for 10 to 250 guests, with rates based on Menu desired.

## SEEING THE NORTHWEST

A modern Travel Bureau, under the able direction of Miss Blankenhorn, affords the visitor every assistance in plans to see the far-famed beauties of the Northwest. All the marvelous scenic beauties of the "Charmed Land" are easily reached from this very central point. Mount Rainier and Mount Baker, The Olympic Peninsula, Puget Sound's innumerable resorts, Vancouver, Victoria and Harrison Hot Springs, B.C.

---

**1934 TARIFF BULLETIN FOR TOUR AGENTS.** This tariff bulletin described Hotel Mayflower to tour agents as, "One of Seattle's newest modern hotels. 12 stories of modern fireproof construction—250 rooms all outside and all with private bath. Unusually beautiful Lounge and Mezzanine. The very center of the smart uptown Shopping and Theatre districts. Within a block of the city's largest Department Stores, and across the street from the Orpheum and famous Seattle Public Market." It goes on to read, "A modern Travel Bureau, under the able direction of Miss Blankenhorn, affords the visitor every assistance in plans to see the far-famed beauties of the Northwest. All the marvelous scenic beauties of the 'Charmed Land' are easily reached from this very central point. Mount Rainier and Mount Baker, The Olympic Peninsula, Puget Sound's innumerable resorts, Vancouver, Victoria and Harrison Hot Springs, BC." (Courtesy of Patricia Walker.)

30

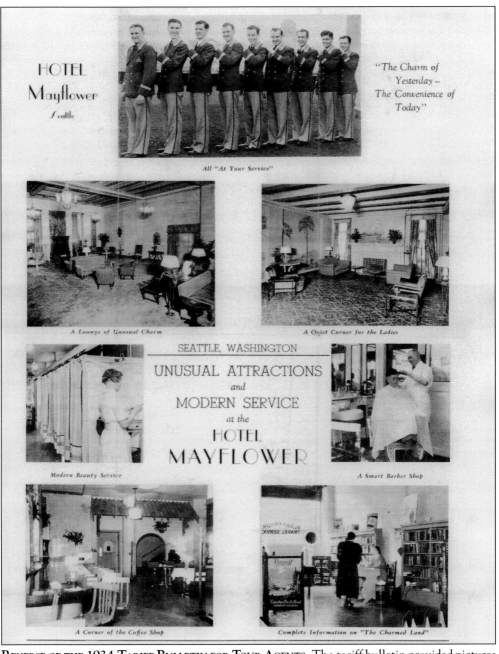

HOTEL
Mayflower
Seattle

"The Charm of
Yesterday –
The Convenience of
Today"

All "At Your Service"

A Lounge of Unusual Charm

A Quiet Corner for the Ladies

SEATTLE, WASHINGTON

UNUSUAL ATTRACTIONS
*and*
MODERN SERVICE
*at the*
HOTEL
MAYFLOWER

Modern Beauty Service

A Smart Barber Shop

A Corner of the Coffee Shop

Complete Information on "The Charmed Land"

REVERSE OF THE 1934 TARIFF BULLETIN FOR TOUR AGENTS. The tariff bulletin provided pictures that highlighted the special features within the Hotel Mayflower. Uniformed bell service of nine was "At your service." The lobby was described as a lounge of "unusual charm." Phil Cook's Barbershop, which had two entrances, one in the lobby and the other on Olive Way, was described as "smart." The mezzanine was described as "a quiet corner for the ladies." Mrs. Galbraith's beauty parlor, located off the mezzanine above the barbershop, was described as "modern." The coffee shop was located down a stairway from the lobby; it too had a door on Olive Way next to the barbershop. The travel bureau, located off the lobby near the Fourth Avenue entrance, was described as providing "complete information on 'The Charmed Land.' " (Courtesy of Patricia Walker.)

**MAYFLOWER'S MODERN KITCHEN ADVERTISEMENT IN HOTEL NEWS OF THE WEST, JUNE 1934.** This advertisement for gas service includes a testimonial touting the benefits of gas by hotel manager R.P. Ward. The included picture at top shows the Mayflower's kitchen, with insulated ovens with thermostat control, a four-deck bake oven, steam table, salamander broiler, and two coffee urn burners. (Courtesy of Seattle Public Library.)

**HOTEL MAYFLOWER'S NEON SIGNS ON THE ROOF.** *Hotel News of the West* reported in November 1935, "The Mayflower is completing the installation of a huge roof neon sign. The letters will be in red and are eight feet high, with an over-all dimension of 52 by 35 feet. Above the sign will be mounted a blue and green border connected with a flasher. The sign was designed and installed by the Campbell Neon Company." Mayflower historians believe that this neon sign was the largest rooftop hotel sign in Seattle. (Courtesy of Museum of History & Industry.)

Mayflower Hotel, Seattle

Charles W. Hunlock succeeds R. Ward as manager of this popular hotel. (See page 11)

**HOTEL NEWS OF THE WEST FRONT PAGE.** The front page of this issue of *Hotel News of the West* states, "Charles W. Hunlock succeeds R. Ward as manager of this popular hotel." Pictured below is Hunlock's employment memo of agreement. *Hotel News of the West* reported in February 1935, "Mr. Hunlock announced that he does not expect to make any drastic changes in the operating policy of the Mayflower, but expects to utilize his connections to increase the transient business of the hotel. He also expects to go after a greater volume of tourist trade." Hunlock was general manager for 14 years from 1935 to 1948. He was the longest tenured general manager until 2012. (Left, courtesy of Seattle Public Library; below, courtesy Manuscripts, Archives, and Special Collections, Washington State University Libraries.)

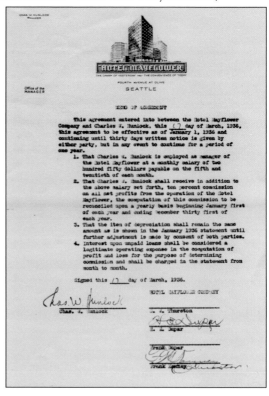

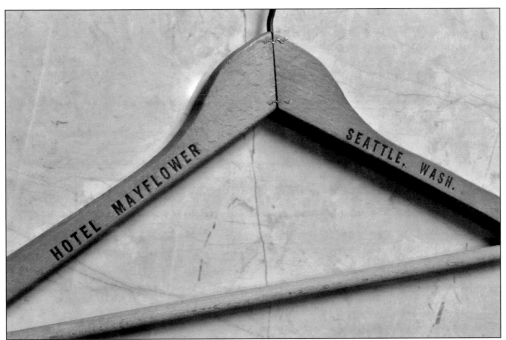

HOTEL MAYFLOWER HANGER AND HOTEL MAYFLOWER MATCHBOOK. Both hangers and matchbooks were very common items that featured the Hotel Mayflower's logo. A grandson who loved his grandmother very much shared this Mayflower memory, "When I was cleaning out my Grandmother's closet I came across a hanger that had 'Hotel Mayflower, Seattle, Wash.' stamped on it. When I asked my Grandmother about it, her response was, 'Oh, I loved that place.' After she peacefully passed away, I thought it best to return it to the hotel where it had come . . . she took very good care of it for seventy five years!" (Above, courtesy of Eric Cooley.)

**Mr. and Mrs. Harry Brown**

request the honor of your presence at the

wedding reception of their daughter

**Sally Sue**

to

**William M. Walker**

Sunday Evening, January thirtieth,

nineteen hundred and thirty-eight

at nine o'clock

The Terrace Room

Mayflower Hotel

Seattle, Washington

Bride's Residence
932 29th Avenue

THE WALKERS' WEDDING AND 50TH ANNIVERSARY INVITATIONS. Both events were held at the Mayflower. Sally Sue Walker said, "We were married at the Mayflower in your then Terrace Room on January 30, 1938. We celebrated our 50th anniversary on January 30, 1988, in your now Pilgrim Room—one and the same. It was a super party—your staff was outstanding in their accommodation and service. Many thanks for fond memories." In the 1930s, the Terrace Room was decorated in buff, henna, and sea-green colors, which effectively evoked a touch of the Renaissance. Its comprehensive collection of authentic antiques was comprised of pictures, statuary, and beautiful glassware. (Both, courtesy of Sally Sue and William Walker.)

**Mr. and Mrs. William Walker**

request the honor of your presence at their

**Fiftieth Wedding Anniversary**

Saturday Evening, January thirtieth

nineteen hundred and eighty-eight

at seven o'clock

The Pilgrim Room

Mayflower Hotel

Fourth and Olive

Seattle, Washington

R.S.V.P.
by January 15th
(206) 322-2455

Attire: Vintage 1930
Cocktails and Dinner
No presents please

**1930s Hotel Mayflower Brochure Showing Coffee Shop, Lobby, Mezzanine, and Guest Rooms.** The following is a Mayflower-related memory, "Beginning in 1930s, my father, druggist and businessman of Petersburg, Alaska, may have been one of the oldest and most frequent guests at the Mayflower. He made many trips, traveling back and forth two to three times a year. It was his home-away-from-home, . . . being so centrally located and loved its convenience. If you could visit our home in the north-end of Seattle I believe you would be most pleasantly surprised to find that our guest bedroom is called the Mayflower Blue Room, mainly because it is completely furnished with Mayflower furniture that my father purchased from the hotel."

THE CHARM OF YESTERDAY • THE CONVENIENCE OF TODAY

*The Coffee Shop*
Modern . . . . Attractive

*The Lounge and Mezzanine*
Spacious . . . Restful

*Single Rooms*
from $3.00 a day
Quiet - Convenient - Livable

*Double Rooms*
from $4.00 a day
Twin beds from $5.00 a day

**HOTEL MAYFLOWER COFFEE SHOP IN 1938.** *Hotel News of the West* reported in March 1938, "Continuing to operate every day during the modernization, the coffee shop is now completely redone, and is a cheerful, inviting place in which to eat. With a color scheme of cream and red, the room presents a most attractive picture, from the new recessed and mirrored back bar of the counter to the protected alcove of convenient booths. New drapes of woven cloth frame the windows which are further enhanced by the new Venetian blinds." (Courtesy of Museum of History & Industry, PEMCO Webster & Stevens Collection.)

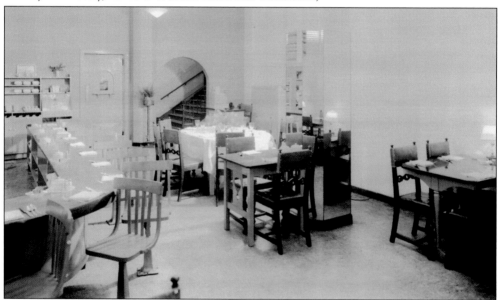

**HOTEL MAYFLOWER COFFEE SHOP IN 1938.** *Hotel News of the West* reported in March 1938, "All furniture has been refinished and some new pieces installed and there are comfortable seats for every patron, whether they prefer the lowboy counter, a table or one of the booths." One coffee shop patron stated, "I worked at the Chas. E. Sullivan Florist across the street from the Mayflower. Our favorite lunch place was the counter in the coffee shop where everybody knew each other." (Courtesy of Museum of History & Industry, PEMCO Webster & Stevens Collection.)

**HOTEL MAYFLOWER POSTCARDS.** This beautifully detailed watercolor postcard of the hotel's exterior is very similar to the postcards used for the Bergonian Hotel. Noted differences include the American flag on the roof and a large six-story neon sign on the northwest corner of the hotel. The postcard depicts a city scene at Fourth Avenue where Olive Way and Stewart Street meet. Directly across the street from the Hotel Mayflower is the Times Square Building, built in 1916. Across the street from the Times Square Building is the Centennial Building, built in 1925. The intersection of Fourth Avenue, Olive Way, and Stewart Street along with the buildings noted still remains.

HOTEL MAYFLOWER — SEATTLE, WASHINGTON

**WESTERN HOTEL EMPLOYEE MAGAZINE (WHEM).** In 1941, Hotel Mayflower was one of 14 hotels managed by Western Hotels Inc. The operating staff of all the hotels totaled around 1,500 and a company newsletter was created. Hotel Mayflower employee Van Hewitt was quoted as saying in the April 1941 edition, "I think the publication of an employees' magazine a splendid step to further closer cooperation among ourselves and the organization for which we work, and sincerely hope everyone will take a personal interest in it so that it may have a long and prosperous life." (Courtesy of Manuscripts, Archives, and Special Collections, Washington State University Libraries.)

**WORLD WAR II.** One guest remembered, "It was in the midst of World War II and we eloped on the Kirkland Ferry just two days before my husband was to report to duty. We went to Seattle and the Hotel Mayflower. The staff was thoughtful and kind to us, acting like they hardly noticed that we were a happy, nervous young couple trying to hide the fact that we were newlyweds in the middle of a war. Almost fifty years later we are healthy, happy and sassy and have special feelings for the Mayflower of 1943." (Both, courtesy of Manuscripts, Archives, and Special Collections, Washington State University Libraries.)

# TWO LUMPS FOR VICTORY

So says Veda Anderson, waitress at the Mayflower, to Jack Stansberry, defense worker en route to Alaska. "Sugar might win the war," says Veda. "If we cut down consumption enough to make sufficient ammunition. Why, it takes an acre and seven-tenths to fire one shell from a sixteen-inch gun. So from now on we'll all watch the sugar bowl."

Stansberry was convinced by Veda's story and therefore took only two lumps, when he had usually taken six before.

Veda also drives slowly to save gasoline and tires, and often walks to work to further curtail wear and tear on her car.

"We all have a job to do," says she, "so, let's do it—NOW!"

*Warn customers about hot dishes*

---

**Whem**
WESTERN HOTELS EMPLOYEES MAGAZINE

Volume II    APRIL, 1943    Number 2

### LET'S ALL DO OUR PART

Buy Wisely ★ Eat Wisely
Maintain Good Health
Take Good Care of Things
Waste Nothing ★ Do Not
Hoard ★ Aid Salvaging
Buy War Bonds and
Stamps ★ Stop Rumors

WESTERN **W** HOTELS INC.

# UNITED STATES TREASURY DEPARTMENT

*For patriotic cooperation rendered in behalf of the*

*War Finance Program this citation is awarded to*

## Mayflower Hotel

*Given under my hand and seal on* **Oct. 20th,** *19* **44**

*Henry Morgenthau Jr.*

SECRETARY OF THE TREASURY

SURPASSED
**HOTEL
QUOTA**
A BOND SALE FOR EVERY HOTEL ROOM
5TH WAR LOAN DRIVE

**US Treasury Department Certificate of Patriotic Cooperation.** *Hotel News of the West* reported on January 1, 1945, that the Mayflower was among 26 Washington hotels to receive a special citation from the US Treasury Department for meeting their quota of a $500 bond sale for every guest room during the Fifth War Loan. (Courtesy of Randy Dixon.)

**GREAT NORTHERN GOAT NEON SIGN NORTH OF THE HOTEL MAYFLOWER ON THE ROOF OF THE CENTENNIAL BUILDING.** One Mayflower guest shared the following Great Northern Goat–related memory, "During my husband's furlough during WWII, my parents gave a brunch reception at the Hotel Mayflower after an early morning wedding. Our room looked at a large flashing sign of the Great Northern Goat. When the sign was on our room was completely illuminated. When it was off, the room was in total darkness. I being the only child, my mother was not ready to accept the fact I was a married woman. Later that evening, my mother had asked to see the room that my parents had paid for. After entering she sat down and refused to leave. She had to be forcibly removed by my father. We joked that my mother must have chosen this room with the flashing sign so that there would be someone to stand guard all night." (Courtesy of Museum of History & Industry.)

**HOTEL MAYFLOWER AT NIGHT WITH RED NEON SIGN ON ROOF.** A hired contractor shared the following about the Mayflower, "Just after WWII, I was working for a neon sign company that was hired by the Hotel Mayflower to put the large neon roof sign in working order. The sign had been turned off during the war due to blackout orders. It was necessary to make many trips from the service truck to the roof to take up tools and supplies for the job. Every time I would call for the elevator I would have the same beautiful girl operator. There were two elevators. No matter which elevator came, when the door opened, it was the same girl. I was very perplexed how this could be. The mystery was solved when both elevators came at the same time. The hotel had identical twin elevator operators." This image is of the same scene as that on the cover of the book. (Courtesy of *Seattle Times*.)

## BILL OF SALE
#### BY CORPORATION

Know All Men by These Presents, THAT THE BARTELL DRUG COMPANY, a Washington corporation,

of ____City of Seattle_____County of_____King_____,

State of____Washington_____, the first party, for and in consideration of the sum

of_ ONE THOUSAND TWO HUNDRED FOUR AND NO/100_____Dollars,

lawful money of the United States of America, to it in hand paid by_ HOTEL MAYFLOWER CO., a

_____Washington corporation_____ of__City of Seattle_____

the second part_Y___, the receipt whereof is hereby acknowledged, does by these presents grant,

bargain, sell and deliver unto the second part__Y___, the following described personal property now

located at_Bartell Drug Store No.13_____ by At 1634 Fourth Avenue, in City of Seattle

in the County of_____King_____and State of_____Washington_____, to-wit:

```
1 Arnold number 17 malted milk mixer, serial number 714396
1 Hamilton number 33 malted milk mixer, serial number 7523
1 Hamilton number 33 malted milk mixer, serial number 7536
1 Hamilton number 18 malted milk mixer, serial number 18M194993
1 30 gallon fountain, single draft station
1 Two well sink and board.
1 3 shelf glass pie case. (Perkins Glass & Fixture Co.)
1 T. J. Topper 2 gallon coffee urn, serial number 12947
1 3 well steam table.
1 Electric steam table, covered.
1 Toastmaster 4 slice toaster serial number 29081
1 Silverware tray.
1 Lacy Products Co. hot cup serial number 46763
1 Complete 14 stool counter and backbar.
1 Liquid Carbonic carbonator, serial number 1804823, complete with pressure gage. ✓
1 Refrigerator box, wooden, with 1/3 horse power compressor unit. ✓
1 Compressor, Water Cooled, with ½ horse power motor.
1 Compressor, Water Cooled, with ½ horse power motor
1 Vaculator stove, 2 burner.
1 Sunkist orange juicer
```

successors

TO HAVE AND TO HOLD the same to the second part__Y___, _____its/___Executors, administrators and assigns forever. And the first party, for itself, and its successors, covenants and agrees to and with the second part__Y___, its successors_____executors x administrators and assigns, that the first party is owner of the said property, goods and chattels and has good right and authority to sell the same, and that it will warrant and defend the sale hereby made unto the second part__Y its successors_____executors x administrators and assigns, against all and every person or persons whomsoever, lawfully claiming or to claim the same,_____

IN WITNESS WHEREOF, the first party has caused its corporate name and seal to be hereto affixed by its officers thereto lawfully authorized on the_____27th_____ day of

July_____19 46.

THE BARTELL DRUG COMPANY

Signed, Sealed and Delivered in the presence of

By_ George Bartell _____
President

Attest: H. C. Morrison _____
Secretary

**BARTELL DRUGS CLOSES 4TH AND OLIVE LOCATION.** Bartell Drugs No. 13 operated at the Hotel Mayflower until 1946. The hotel purchased the entire soda fountain inventory, which included items such as a 30-gallon fountain, single-draft station, well sink and board, complete 14-stool counter, and back bar. This is an important part of Hotel Mayflower history because two years later, when Washington State Initiative 171 passed authorizing the sale of cocktails, the Hotel Mayflower already had a bar in place. This expedited the transition from a soda fountain to a cocktail lounge, resulting in the Hotel Mayflower being the first hotel in Seattle to open a cocktail lounge. It is unclear what occupied the space between the closing of Bartell Drugs No. 13 and the opening of Seattle's first hotel cocktail lounge; however, records indicate that for a short time the space was identified as the Polka-Dot Room. (Courtesy of Manuscripts, Archives, and Special Collections, Washington State University Libraries.)

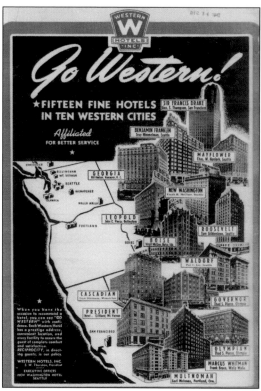

"Go Western!" This 1950 advertisement is for Western Hotels Inc. and its "fifteen fine hotels in ten Washington cities." A past Mayflower employee shared, "During those great old days at the Mayflower, it was owned and operated by Western Hotels. The manager of the hotel was George Marble, the son-in-law of S.W. Thurston, who owned Western Hotels. Bill Hewitt was Assistant Manager, who later created Tillicum Village on Blake Island State Park. William Keithan was Catering Manager, later Assistant Manager and was one of the most capable and intelligent people it has ever been my pleasure to know." (Both, courtesy of Seattle Public Library.)

**WOMEN DISCUSSING FEMININE VIEWPOINT AT HOTEL MAYFLOWER.** *Front!* magazine in summer 1947 reported, "Hotel operations get a good working over from the feminine viewpoint whenever this group meets for lunch in Seattle. These women watch over coffee shop, dining room and banquet affairs at their respective hotels." (Courtesy of Manuscripts, Archives, and Special Collections, Washington State University Libraries.)

**HOTEL MAYFLOWER BELLMEN UNIFORMS.** *Hotel News of the West* reported on February 1, 1948, "The designs are in line with the latest trend toward a distinctive uniform, which stands out as an identifying mark in the entire hotel group. The coats are a wine-maroon with collars, cuffs and trousers of special-dyed gray-green. Cuffs and collars are trimmed with gold braid." (Courtesy of Manuscripts, Archives, and Special Collections, Washington State University Libraries.)

**Hotel Manager George Marble on Steps in Hotel Mayflower with Children.** *Front!* magazine in May 1952 reported, "Mayflower among the first to take advantage of Western Hotels' new Family Plan where wives and children of American soldiers are encouraged to travel. Development of low priced 'kiddies' plates' to satisfy the children's tastes and needs." The article further explained this lobby scene, "Five children were playing hide and seek among the upholstered chairs. One mother with four sons (the oldest about eleven) was busy herding her tribe past the desk to check them out. There were kids all over the place! Mrs. Melvin Fulkerson, whose husband is a sergeant in Japan, was happy to hear that the Mayflower had this Family Plan. She said that the Mayflower treats them so nice, unlike other hotels that just tolerate them." (Courtesy of Manuscripts, Archives, and Special Collections, Washington State University Libraries.)

**Tony Dortero, Longtime Front Desk Agent at Hotel Mayflower.** A past employee shared this memory, "The Front Desk was directly across from the elevators and was very small. One person acted as both clerk and cashier. The switchboard stood against the wall that covered what is now the entrance to Oliver's and was the old fashioned type with a plug for each room." (Courtesy of Joyce Dortero Schell.)

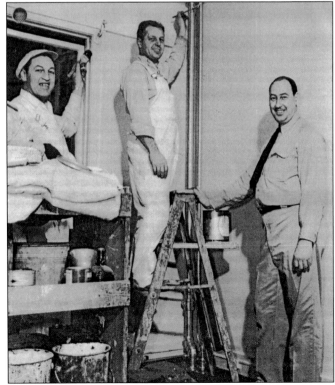

**Maintenance Staff at the Hotel Mayflower.** *Front!* magazine reported, "By the end of 1950, it had completely remodeled 89 rooms and the pace is still continuing. One innovation at the Mayflower is a heating system that preheats a lower grade oil. The money saved by burning the lower-cost oil paid for installation the first year it was used." (Courtesy of Manuscripts, Archives, and Special Collections, Washington State University Libraries.)

**WESTERN HOTEL COCKTAIL LOUNGES, 1949.** Hotel Mayflower opened Western Hotels' first cocktail lounge. *Front!* magazine reported, "The management of the Mayflower forsook history and chose the name 'Carousel Room' for its cocktail lounge. Little merry-go-rounds will form the decorative motif. It will be a small, cozy lounge located in the space formerly occupied by the Polka-Dot Shop." (Courtesy of Manuscripts, Archives, and Special Collections, Washington State University Libraries.)

**CAROUSEL ROOM AT THE HOTEL MAYFLOWER, 1952.** *Front!* magazine reported in January 1952, "Just in time for the Christmas season, the Mayflower opened Seattle's lively cocktail lounge December 17. Named The Carousel, it is an expanded and greatly elaborated upon version of the original Carousel opened by the hotel." (Courtesy of Manuscripts, Archives, and Special Collections, Washington State University Libraries.)

**CHEF CLEM SUMMERFIELD OF THE CAROUSEL ROOM.** *Front!* magazine in April 1953 reported, "The Hotel Mayflower won a bronze medal award for original display with a replica of the lively Carousel made by Chef Clem Summerfield. The top of the merry-go-round was made of icing, as were the base and side trimmings. The seat close to the pole was made of jello and the chairs were of cookie dough. The Mayflower also won another bronze medal for an assortment of fine hors d'oeuvres. Benjamin Franklin Hotel, Hotel Mayflower, Roosevelt Hotel and Winthrop Hotel, all Western Hotels, walked off with prizes for the food displays at the Exhibit of Culinary Arts in Seattle on February 21, 1953. The show was sponsored by a committee representing the entire food industry in the area and was seen by more than four thousand people." (Courtesy of Manuscripts, Archives, and Special Collections, Washington State University Libraries.)

**SEAFAIR PRINCESS LUNCHEON.** In August 1952, the Seafair Princess Luncheon took place at the Hotel Mayflower, as seen above. Pictured at left, Carousel Room employees are enjoying Seafair Week. *Front!* magazine reported, "It is tradition during Seafair week in Seattle that bold, marauding Pirates take over the city and rule it with a free hand. Shown raiding the Mayflower's treasure chest are members of the hotel crew." Seafair began as a plan to celebrate Seattle's centennial in 1951–1952. The first Seafair Grand Parade was on Saturday, August 12, 1950. (Above, courtesy of Forde Photographers; left, courtesy of Manuscripts, Archives, and Special Collections, Washington State University Libraries.)

**MISS GOOD MORNING.** *Front!* magazine in September 1954 reported, "Miss Good Morning, Mary Martin, a Hotel Mayflower Coffee Shop waitress, was one of 48 finalists judged in Chicago in a contest sponsored by the Kellogg Company. Mrs. Martin wrote an essay that won her the Washington State prize of a clock radio and a $25 savings bond. She was one of 35,000 restaurant employees who participated in the contest." (Courtesy of Manuscripts, Archives, and Special Collections, Washington State University Libraries.)

**WHALE MURAL IN THE COFFEE SHOP AT THE HOTEL MAYFLOWER.** A Mayflower guest stated, "In the 1950s, my mother and I would take the bus downtown and as a special treat, we would have breakfast at the Hotel Mayflower Coffee Shop. And, oh, how I remember those sumptuous waffles and the painted mural." (Courtesy of Manuscripts, Archives, and Special Collections, Washington State University Libraries.)

Western Hotels, Inc.

*Front!*

JULY, 1954
Vol. 8, No. 3

MISS GOOD MORNING _____ Page 3

**HOTEL MAYFLOWER COFFEE SHOP ADVERTISING SIGNS.** *Front!* magazine reported, "The Hotel Mayflower Coffee Shop in Seattle fronts on Olive Way, one of the heaviest pedestrian-traveled streets in the city. Recognizing the great advertising potential of the location, the hotel food staff developed a series of signs that are changed regularly for the passing public." (Courtesy of Manuscripts, Archives, and Special Collections, Washington State University Libraries.)

**BUSBOYS.** *Front!* magazine in September 1954 reported, "The Brockman cousins attend Queen Anne High School in Seattle, and have worked as Bus Boys part-time at the Mayflower for three years. Their tumbling prowess may come in mighty handy during a possible future career in hotel work." (Courtesy of Manuscripts, Archives, and Special Collections, Washington State University Libraries.)

**WESTERN HOTELS SELLS HOTEL MAYFLOWER TO ACQUIRE OLYMPIC HOTEL.** *Front!* magazine reported in 1955, "Sale of the 225 room Mayflower in Seattle, which had been a Western Hotel for more than 20 years, was announced June 18 by S.W. Thurston. The Doric Company is the new owner." The sale of the Hotel Mayflower and the New Washington to the Doric Company was a key component to the purchase of the Olympic by Western Hotels. (Courtesy of Manuscripts, Archives, and Special Collections, Washington State University Libraries.)

**DORIC HOTEL COMPANY BUYS HOTEL MAYFLOWER.** *Pacific Northwest Hotel News* in August 1956 reported, "There's a new star in the hotel scene in the West—the Doric Hotel Company, which in a few short years has acquired and tied together a group of top hotels to make it one of the major hospitality organizations on the Pacific coast. Floyd Clodfelter is dominant figure in the formation of Doric." (Courtesy of Seattle Public Library.)

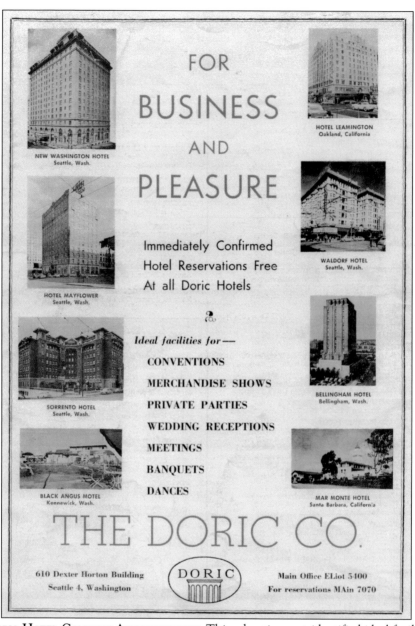

**THE DORIC HOTEL COMPANY ADVERTISEMENT.** This advertisement identified ideal facilities for conventions, merchandise shows, private parties, wedding receptions, meetings, banquets, and dances. Joyce Dortero Schell shared this Mayflower memory, "In the 1950s, my father, Tony Dortero [pictured on page 49], worked at the Mayflower for over ten years. I remember when the Seattle baseball team, the Rainiers, were in town and staying at the Mayflower. The coach would give Dad tickets to the games. I remember when Dad made arrangements to reserve one of the third- or fourth-floor hotel rooms in the summer, facing Fourth Avenue, so we could watch the Seafair Parade from the open windows. I remember when I was in high school and families that stayed at the Mayflower Hotel would often request babysitters. One time I was babysitting, one of the Seafair Pirates came in and pretended to kidnap me. The kids thought the pirates were great. The Mayflower Hotel holds a special place in my heart." (Courtesy of Seattle Public Library.)

**MAYFLOWER HOTEL BROCHURE.** Shortly after the Doric Hotel Company took ownership, the name was changed to the Mayflower Hotel, and lobby renovations included moving the front desk from across the elevators back into the lobby where it was originally located prior to 1933. The front desk was modern with white tufted coverings. A brochure explained the hotel to have an "air of comfortable refinement and sensible prices well within your budget. Attractive and comfortable rooms to relax and enjoy every convenience and luxury. Located in the heart of downtown Seattle, close to stores, theaters, night clubs and fine restaurants. Free courtesy car transportation between airline, train, bus and steamship terminals."

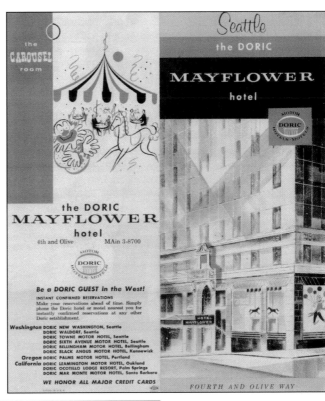

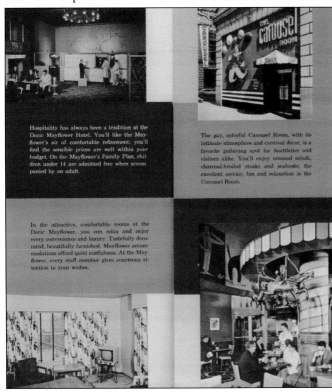

**THE DORIC COMPANY ADVERTISEMENTS.**
The Doric Company was trendsetting in its marketing efforts. These advertisements highlight the company's creative approach to capturing the attention of the traveling public. The following is an example, "Travel Doric, travel light . . . All Credit cards are accepted at every Doric Hotel!" The Doric Company also advertised its restaurants and lounges using matchbook covers, a creative approach in identifying the unique attributes of these facilities. These marketing efforts reinforced the Doric Company culture, as reported in *Pacific Northwest Hotel News* in August 1956, "Where their hotels and motels are not looked upon as a chain in any sense of the word. The view is of running an organization that heightens each property's individual charm and atmosphere." (Both, courtesy of Seattle Public Library.)

**MAYFLOWER MEN'S STYLING SALON, 1960.** "That's my chair!" said Birney Dempcy, a regular customer of the barbershop. E. Schleiger, daughter of salon owners Hugh and Macel Elkins, remembered, "The salon was one of the first in Seattle to have wall-to-wall carpeting and operated on an appointment basis. They offered discreet services, such as permanents and coloring. The elite service attracted customers like Mr. Best, Mr. Loomis, the Nordstroms and officers of local companies." Hugh Elkins retired in 1982, making him the last proprietor of the barbershop, which had been in operation since the hotel opened in 1927. (Both, courtesy of E. Schleiger.)

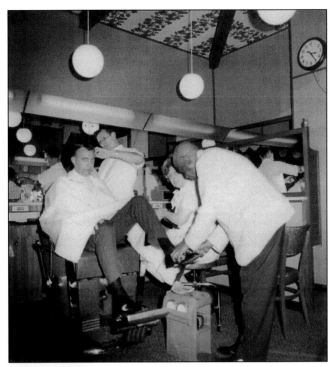

CLODFELTER & BOWDEN
ATTORNEYS AT LAW
610 DEXTER HORTON BUILDING
SEATTLE 4, WASHINGTON
MUTUAL 2-1163

WARREN V. CLODFELTER
ALLEN A. BOWDEN
JAMES V. O'CONNER
BIRNEY N. DEMPCY

March 28, 1961

Mr. Harry Henke, Jr.
1020 Norton Building
Seattle 4, Washington

Dear Mr. Henke:

Please find enclosed the documents involved in the assignment of interests in the Doric Mayflower Hotel.

We would appreciate receiving the consent of Pacific Hotels, Inc. to these Assignments.

Very truly yours,

CLODFELTER & BOWDEN

By _Birney N. Dempcy_
Birney N. Dempcy

BND:jb
Encls.

SELLING THE HOTEL. Birney Dempcy, a young attorney with the Clodfelter and Bowden law firm, was given the assignment to assist Floyd Clodfelter in selling the hotel. This letter was the first step in the process that led to negotiations with the Gene Autry Hotel Company. Birney was given a bungalow suite at the Ocotillo Lodge in Palm Springs as his headquarters to negotiate the sale. He remembers the assignment having the added benefit of "partying with the stars." Marie Dempcy remembers the assignment differently, "He did not! He worked twelve to fourteen hours a day." After Autry's representatives inspected all of the hotels, it was decided to purchase only two: the Ocotillo Lodge in Palm Springs, California, and what is now the Andaz West Hollywood by Hyatt Hotels on Sunset Boulevard in Hollywood, California. Later, the Motel Development Company, whose principals were former Doric Company employees, purchased the Mayflower Hotel. In 1972, the mortgage company foreclosed on the property. This was the second time in its history that the Mayflower went into foreclosure. (Courtesy of Manuscripts, Archives, and Special Collections, Washington State University Libraries.)

# *Three*

# "QUITE SIMPLY, ONE OF A KIND"
## 1973 TO PRESENT

In 1973, Birney Dempcy, as general partner, formed a limited partnership to purchase the hotel out of foreclosure. This was the only purchase offer that the mortgage company had received in over a year.

As Birney recalls, he came home one night and told his wife, Marie, "I bought a hotel today!" Marie went down to look at this purchase and nearly cried because the hotel had been so neglected and was in such bad repair.

Renovation began almost immediately, and as new furniture started to arrive, Birney asked Marie to oversee its installation. Marie agreed to come in for this one project only; however, as the work progressed, she fell in love with the hotel's emerging charm and became dedicated to its operation and restoration.

Shortly after they took ownership, "Park" was added to the hotel's name in anticipation of Westlake Park, which officially opened in 1988. The Dempcys soon found out that part of the original City of Seattle's Westlake Center Plan included the demolition of the hotel. The Dempcys challenged the constitutionality of this condemnation and won. In 1988, after two years of construction, Westlake Center opened with a connecting door on the hotel's mezzanine level. The hotel had (and continues to have) direct indoor access to its boutique shops and the Monorail station leading to the Space Needle. In 2009, the Seattle Light Rail system to SeaTac Airport also added direct access.

In the last 40 years, the Mayflower Park Hotel has been home to many Seattle "firsts." In 1976, Oliver's opened as Seattle's first daylight bar. In 1983, Marie Dempcy became Seattle's first female hotel general manager and, in 1993, was elected by the board as the first woman to chair the Seattle–King County Convention and Visitors Bureau. In 1997, the Mayflower Park Hotel became Seattle's first member of Historic Hotels of America. In 1998, Paul Ishii became the first ethnic minority general manager in Seattle. In 2012, Paul Ishii became the longest tenured general manager of the Mayflower Park Hotel. That same year he was the first ethnic minority and first hotel general manager to be elected as president of Seattle Rotary No. 4. Seattle Rotary was founded in 1909 and holds the distinction of being the largest Rotary organization in the world.

"The transition of bringing the hotel to its present-day reputation was a day-by-day process. It is not easy to take a seedy hotel with a bad reputation and turn that around," recalled Birney Dempcy.

## HOTEL'S CONDITION UPON PURCHASE.
Marie Dempcy recalls the hotel's condition when they took ownership, "In the lobby there was a horrible red carpet with cigarette burns everywhere and a couple of couches with cigarette burns and the stuffing coming out and a tiny television set against a wall on top of a bedside table. The whole place smelled of a cheap perfume that was in the Ladies Room. One would put a nickel in a machine and it sprayed the perfume. It was a dump!"

**1974 LOG BOOK.** The following log book entries describe the hotel's condition further, "Police recommend we write to the Mayor requesting he take action to control downtown prostitution;" "Nearly froze to death. No heat in Coffee Shop either;" "Windows still stuck open and one glass is broken in Room 707;" and "Called police to ticket cars in front of hotel. No place left for cabs or guest loading. We do not owe free parking to any pimp in town."

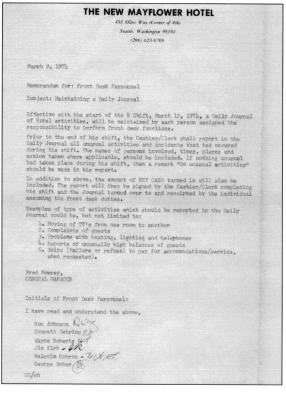

**BASEMENT WITH EXPOSED SPRINKLERS.**
"Unfortunately, the sprinklers were put
in upside down," recalls Marie Dempcy.
"The main reason we got a good price
on the hotel is because the mortgage
company had gotten notice from the fire
marshal that the hotel would be closed
if the sprinkler system was not installed.
They did not want to put any more money
into the hotel," stated Birney Dempcy.

**A MAYFLOWER HOTEL GUEST ROOM AT
TIME OF PURCHASE.** Polly Lane of *Seattle
Times* reported on May 8, 1974, that a
"facelift [was] under way on Mayflower
Hotel. A half million dollar refurbishing
and name change are planned for the 47
year old hotel. Remodeling is planned
in at least two phases, with the first to
be completed by June 1. Initial work
includes remodeling of one hundred
guest rooms and all the corridors."

## MAYFLOWER PARK HOTEL

4th & Olive Way, Seattle, Washington 98101
(206) 623-8700

# 8 to 8 for $8

## A Holiday Gift from the Mayflower Park Hotel

BE OUR GUEST
from 8 a.m. until 8 p.m. for $8.00

SHOPPING for the day? Attending a matinee at the Seattle Center? Whatever brings you to downtown Seattle for just the day, consider being our guest for 12 hours.

THE MAYFLOWER PARK HOTEL is located in the heart of Seattle, where you can ride a free bus to historic Pioneer Square or walk a few blocks to the famed Public Market. Fine shops and department stores surround us and we are the closest hotel to the Monorail Terminal which connects to the Seattle Center with year-around special events and entertaining attractions.

Valid until Feb. 29, 1976

"BE OUR GUEST." The Mayflower invited people to be its guest from 8:00 a.m. until 8:00 p.m. for $8, a creative marketing approach aimed at those spending the day in the city. The back side of the advertisement includes a bonus coupon for overnight parking for hotel guests only.

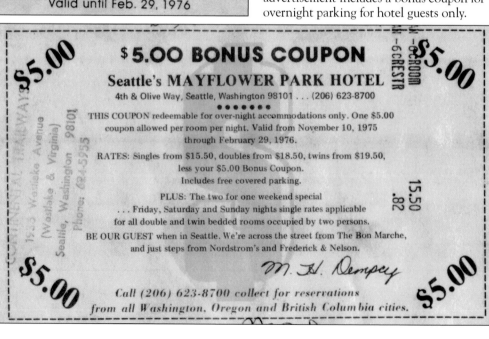

**REMODELED MAYFLOWER.**
Polly Lane of *Seattle Times* reported on June 27, 1976, "The former Carousel Room site was remodeled under new liquor laws as an open bar which means the curtains can be opened on the newly installed paned-windows to offer views down the street. Remodeling, directed by Marie Dempcy, has transformed 135 of the 200 guest rooms into new spaces. Other rooms have been redecorated. Most of the second floor guest rooms [pictured at right] are being converted to meeting and display rooms. There had been some talk of replacing the old hotel structure with a new high-rise building but the cost was considered prohibitive and the work undertaken by the Dempcys made it more compatible with the new development."

**RENOVATIONS.** Lars Henry Ringseth from the *Seattle Weekly* reported on August 4, 1976, "Two years ago the decline showed definite signs of reversal. The lobby was completely revamped, the offices remodeled, and an entrance on Fourth Avenue was opened, providing the hotel with a much needed aperture to the west. Many of the 200 rooms were tastefully remodeled, and the light red brick exterior was cleaned. The Mayflower Park Hotel is fast becoming a very good idea in Seattle: a smaller, medium-priced, full service hotel operating independent of a large chain. By now, 165 of the rooms have been completely redecorated and refurnished. The remaining 35 have been painted and furnished with the best of the hotel's old furniture. In the Mayflower's half-century history is added evidence that the Mayflower Park is an idea whose time has come."

**NORTHWEST VIEW.** The following excerpt is from an article by Jim Faber in a special women's issue of *Northwest View* in January 1977, "What do Art History and Hotel Management have in common? The restoration of the Mayflower Park Hotel. Marie Dempcy, Assistant Manager of the Mayflower Park, came to her post at the 200-room hostelry with credentials that include three years as a University of Washington Art Major, a mother of four, and wife of an attorney who joined up with nine doctors and two businessmen to buy the aging hotel and bring it back to life. Today, three years after Birney Dempcy and his associates purchased the ailing Mayflower, the restored hotel has created its own niche. She started out three years ago saying she would fill in for a few months, and the job got into her blood. Today her duties range from decorating the Mayflower Park's seventeen-foot lobby Christmas tree to consulting with Architects Kumatra and Mesher on decorating. She also interviews job applicants and manages Oliver's. To date she's pleased with the results, despite three years of headaches."

**NEW SUITES.** Marie Dempcy said, "These were our brand new suites in 1976 and the first remodel of the rooms after we bought the hotel. We couldn't afford a professional model, so this picture of me was used at the airport alongside other hotels advertising to the incoming passengers at Seattle International Airport. The carpet was orange shag, the latest thing then. Those chairs were used in Oliver's first remodel, which was a great success. In fact, Birney purchased those white chairs before the color concept of Oliver's was decided." In 1976, room rates were $17.50 for a single bed; $22.50 for two twin beds; and $22.50 for a double bed.

**GUEST ROOMS AT THE MAYFLOWER PARK HOTEL.** Jim Faber of *Northwest View* in January 1977 reported, "Today, approximately 80 percent of the two hundred rooms have been redecorated and refurnished in a simple warm décor. Fabrics and carpeting are in muted tones. Walls in the rooms are bare, save for a pair of framed abstract paintings by Seattle artist Joseph Delatore. The only visible remnants of the past are a few bathrooms still retaining the pleasing old hexagon tiles of the twenties." Every decorative feature of the room was coordinated, including the artwork, bedspread, upholstery, and carpet.

**MAYFLOWER PARK HOTEL HOUSEKEEPING STAFF.** Every decorative feature of the hotel was coordinated, including hotel uniforms. The housekeeping uniforms were custom designed to coordinate with the guest room décor. This theme continued to the stationery, which was designed using the same brown tones. To make sure no detail was overlooked, the ink in the pens was brown. The front desk uniforms were chosen to coordinate with the lobby. Brenda Bible, the room attendant pictured at left, is a longtime employee, having recently celebrated her 32nd anniversary with the hotel. Her current title is housekeeping manager. Her mother, Bettye, has worked for the hotel for over 40 years, and her cousin Tony (pictured below) has worked for over 30 years. Combined, that one family has dedicated their careers to the Mayflower Park Hotel, amounting to over 100 years. Tony's motto is "my last look is my guest's first."

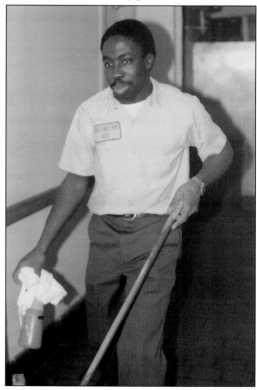

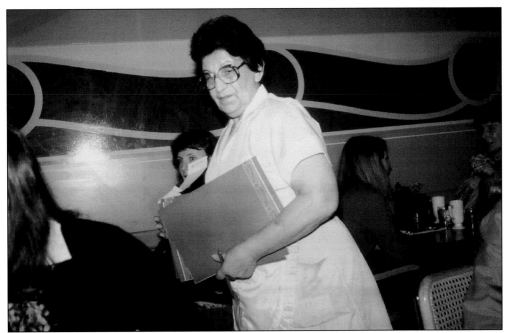

**MAYFLOWER PARK HOTEL COFFEE SHOP.** When the Dempcys took ownership of the hotel, the coffee shop was subcontracted out to the same company that operated the Carousel Room. Closing down the Carousel Room involved also taking over the operations of the coffee shop. Changes were immediate, including top-to-bottom cleanup; new counters, tables, and chairs; matching plates; and painted wall graphics. Jo Smith, the server pictured above, was employed in the coffee shop for many years, and even though she was not the food manager, she literally ran the place. The lower picture shows the graphics painted on the window of the Mayflower Park Hotel Coffee Shop.

**MAYFLOWER PARK HOTEL EXTERIOR.** This picture and postcard show new awnings. The exterior awnings were installed in early 1982. By this time, the hotel was gaining a strong reputation as a highly regarded boutique hotel, and the European awning style was consistent with this theme. The *Seattle Weekly* reported on January 19, 1983, "The Mayflower Park Management decided to design a new logo to symbolize the thorough-going renovation. Somebody noticed the stucco pineapples that stud the building's exterior, researched it and discovered 'the pineapple is the symbol for hospitality.' So there you have it—on the new awnings outside the newly spruced up mini-Grand Hotel vestibules leading to the spacious chandeliered lobby, there is a handsomely styled pineapple."

CLIPPERS AT THE MAYFLOWER PARK HOTEL. Jean Godden, *Post Intelligencer* restaurant critic writes, "The sign on the side of the Mayflower Park Hotel at Fourth and Olive reads, 'Clippers' . . . a fashionable hair salon? A place for tycoons to scissor bond coupons? No, Clippers it turns out is a new full-service restaurant for breakfast, lunch and dinner; a completely updated version of the coffee shop once located on the hotel's ground floor. I mused over Clippers' name. Was not the Mayflower for which the hotel is named some kind of clipper ship? Curiosity consumes. I asked the Manager. Clippers, he revealed, is named for the hotel's barbershop and it 'sounded zippy.' " Clippers operated at this location until 1996. The decorative rod iron sign now hangs beautifully outside the Kathy Casey Food Studios in Ballard, Washington.

**CLIPPERS RESTAURANT.** Clippers at the Mayflower Park Hotel won *Lodging Hospitality* magazine's 1983 Designers Circle Awards Competition for hotel interior design. The magazine wrote that the restaurant was designed by Mesher Shing Associates and noted that the judges "unanimously agreed that the Mayflower Park's restaurant renovation was simple, elegant and very well done. The spatial concept divides the restaurant into two levels with an L-shaped seating area wrapped around a lower level. This creates a focal point between the columns with a built-in credenza for refrigerated wine storage and display of fresh fruits and pastries. Marble counters and brass-accented tabletops resonate richness. Large floral water colors over grass cloth-covered walls underscore the warmth and texture of the Robert Mesher and Pamela Purvis design."

**CLIPPERS.** Geoffrey Ray-Wilcox reported, "You might be tempted to call it a rhapsody on a theme of quiet elegance. The Mayflower Park Hotel prefers to simply call it Clippers. Following two months of renovation, the quaint Seattle inn has opened its doors to perhaps the best downtown luncheon stop that has already captured a national award for interior design. Obviously, quite an improvement from the days of the old coffee and barbershops that once inhabited that intimate corner of the old hotel. The luncheon menu is varied and suited to individual tastes and preferences, a rare find in old fashioned hospitality. The price is extremely moderate compared to other luncheon spots available at the smaller, class hotels. Every aspect is affordably priced and my companion and I enjoyed our lunch and Washington wine for well under $20." The photograph below is of Tony, a longtime employee who graciously looks forward to serving guests breakfast as he has for over 25 years.

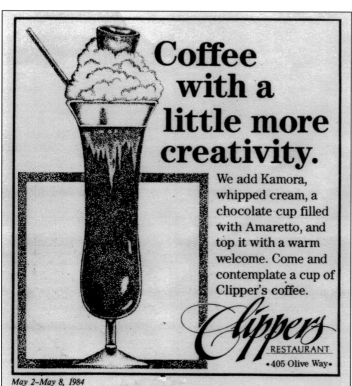

# Coffee with a little more creativity.

We add Kamora, whipped cream, a chocolate cup filled with Amaretto, and top it with a warm welcome. Come and contemplate a cup of Clipper's coffee.

*Clippers*
RESTAURANT
•405 Olive Way•

May 2–May 8, 1984

**CLIPPERS AT THE MAYFLOWER PARK HOTEL.** Advertisements for Clippers Restaurant included creative images and marketing approaches that attracted diners on special occasions.

# Dinner with a little more romance.

Here at Clippers, in a beautifully intimate setting, we provide the elegant mood, the soft music, the sensational food and the thoughtful service perfect for a romantic evening. The rest is up to you.

Reservations ❤ 382-6999
405 Olive Way

*Clippers*
RESTAURANT

**"IT WAS A MONDAY."** It was 1983 when Birney asked Marie to be interim general manager while they went through reorganization. "I agreed, for the interim, and was scared to death. I just was not sure how the staff would react," said Marie Dempcy. How did the staff respond Monday afternoon? They threw a congratulatory party for their new Mayflower Park Hotel interim general manager. On that day, Marie Dempcy became the first female general manager in Seattle. That interim role lasted eight years. In 1993, Marie was elected the first woman to chair the Seattle–King County Convention and Visitors Bureau since its founding in 1956.

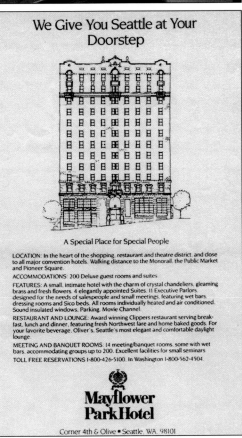

**SHIRT BOARD MARKETING FOR THE MAYFLOWER PARK HOTEL, 1983.** The hotel has always had a strong Canadian following. An advertising approach was introduced using the Madison Shirt Board Company and marketing the hotel to Canadian dry cleaners. A common method of cleaning dress shirts was to bring them to the dry cleaners and have them laundered. These shirts were folded around a cardboard sheet called a shirt board. Instead of having plain shirt boards, the trend at the time was to have advertisements on them, so that when a customer unfolded his shirt, he saw an advertisement of the Mayflower Park Hotel. On the back side of this advertisement was a recipe from Clippers Restaurant.

## FETTUCINI RICARDO

Yield: 4 Servings

**Ingredients:**

> 1 lb. fresh fettucini noodles
> 4 oz. melted butter
> 12 oz. diced chicken breast (raw)
> 3 oz. diced zuccini
> 3 oz. diced onion
> 3 oz. sliced mushrooms
> 1 pinch fresh chopped garlic
> 1½ cups heavy (whipping) cream
> 5 oz. grated parmesan cheese (fresh is recommended)

**Procedure:**

> Boil fresh noodles in salted water for two minutes. Rinse, drain, and set aside. Sauté fresh diced chicken in butter with zuccini, onion, mushrooms and garlic until chicken is cooked through. Add cream and reduce by 1/2. Add parmesan cheese and cook until melted and sauce is a bit thick. Add noodles. Bring back to a boil and remove from heat.
>
> Garnish with grated parmesan cheese and fresh chopped parsley and serve immediately.

*with the compliments of*

### *Mayflower Park Hotel*
### *Clippers Restaurant*
405 OLIVE WAY, SEATTLE, WASHINGTON (206) 623-8700

**OLIVER'S LOUNGE POSTCARD AND GUEST ROOM POSTCARD.** Postcards were created in 1983 to highlight the beautiful features of the hotel. The Dempcys had been involved in the ownership of the hotel for nine years, and by then, the memory of the Mayflower Park Hotel at one time being a neglected hotel was fading. The picture above of Oliver's interior included employees. Looking at the table closest to the windows, wearing a white blouse, is Susan, who, for over 25 years, continues to graciously serve guests in Oliver's. The postcard of a guest room below highlights a suite; colors are red with beige accents.

Mayflower
ParkHotel

405 Olive Way / Seattle, WA 98101
(206) 623-8700

*A Walking Map of Seattle*

MAYFLOWER PARK HOTEL WALKING MAP OF SEATTLE. The location of the Mayflower Park Hotel has always been a valuable feature. Located in the heart of Seattle, the hotel is close to everything that people come to downtown Seattle to enjoy. Open the small brochure and a map opens up, showing a downtown street map with popular Seattle destinations. Creative marketing highlights the hotel's close proximity to the Monorail station, Space Needle, Pike Place Market, Pioneer Square, Smith Tower, Fifth Avenue Theatre, and the International District. Some popular destinations on this map no longer exist, such as the Kingdome and Frederick & Nelson.

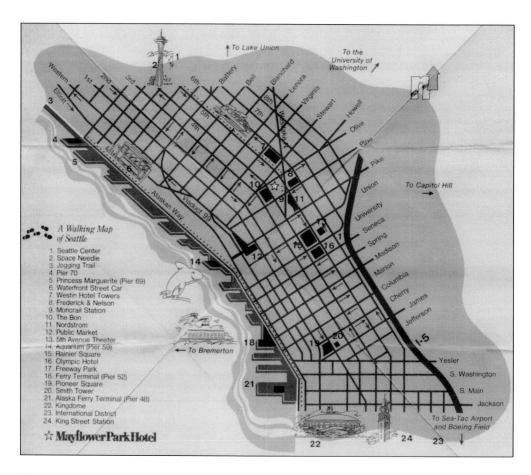

*A Walking Map of Seattle*

1. Seattle Center
2. Space Needle
3. Jogging Trail
4. Pier 70
5. Princess Marguerite (Pier 69)
6. Waterfront Street Car
7. Westin Hotel Towers
8. Frederick & Nelson
9. Monorail Station
10. The Bon
11. Nordstrom
12. Public Market
13. 5th Avenue Theater
14. Aquarium (Pier 59)
15. Rainier Square
16. Olympic Hotel
17. Freeway Park
18. Ferry Terminal (Pier 52)
19. Pioneer Square
20. Smith Tower
21. Alaska Ferry Terminal (Pier 48)
22. Kingdome
23. International District
24. King Street Station

☆ Mayflower Park Hotel

**Lobby Chandelier at the Mayflower Park Hotel.** The chandelier was purchased from the Olympic Hotel in 1980 when it closed for a two-year renovation and sold some of its fixtures. The Dempcys purchased this beautiful chandelier, which originally was located in one of the ballrooms of the hotel. Marie Dempcy, along with Food and Beverage Director Gordon Struck, is cleaning each crystal cylinder prior to installation. This beautiful vintage chandelier was the perfect addition to the hotel lobby, where it remains today. When the Olympic Hotel closed for renovation, the Mayflower Park Hotel became the longest continuously operated hotel in downtown Seattle.

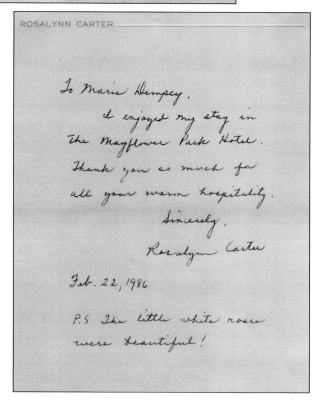

*Pamper yourself...*

At Seattle's most convenient downtown address. Steps away from shopping, theater, sightseeing. Spend a week-end discovering Seattle's amenities, and ours. Ask for our newly remodeled guest rooms, fit for a second honeymoon.

Get away from the regular routine and enjoy each other and Seattle again.

**FIRST LADY ROSALYNN CARTER.** By 1986, the Mayflower Park Hotel was a highly regarded boutique hotel and soon had the honor of anticipating the arrival of First Lady Rosalynn Carter. "What can I do to make the room extra special?" Marie Dempcy recalls. She gave it some thought and purchased a lovely arrangement of white flowers and a beautiful bar of designer soap for the room. Marie Dempcy never personally met the first lady; however, she did receive a lovely note from her.

ROSALYNN CARTER

To Marie Dempcy,

I enjoyed my stay in the Mayflower Park Hotel. Thank you so much for all your warm hospitality.

Sincerely,

Rosalynn Carter

Feb. 22, 1986

P.S. The little white roses were beautiful!

**DEMOLITION FOR WESTLAKE CENTER.** Polly Lane of *Seattle Times* reported on May 8, 1974, "The 12 story, 211 room structure will become the Mayflower Park Hotel to relate to the Westlake Park development being planned by the city, adjoining its south side." Twelve years later demolition began, starting the redevelopment plan that took two years to accomplish. All the buildings between Fourth and Fifth Avenues, Olive Way, and Pine Street were demolished except the Mayflower Park Hotel and Sherman Clay. "It was a dusty mess," recalls Marie Dempcy. Don Tewkesbury of *Post Intelligencer* reported on February 4, 1987, "The Mayflower stands relatively isolated—with the construction project abutting it on the east and south. The only access is from Fourth and Olive. 'I think people are having a harder time getting here. The limited access has caused the January food and beverage business to be down more than normal. We are hoping the construction firm will put in covered sidewalks as soon as they are able. In the meantime, we are trying to be as cooperative and patient as we can be,' said Marie Dempcy, Mayflower General Manager."

**WESTLAKE CENTER.** The center opened on October 20, 1988. *Sunset* magazine in February 1989 reported, "After decades of debate and two years of construction, Seattle's new Westlake Center opened in October to huzzas from the public. Seattleites have enthusiastically taken to the new complex, adopting it as the missing "people place" long yearned for in the center of downtown. It includes a four-level shopping arcade, new Monorail terminal, a score of eateries, and across Pine Street a wedge shaped pocket park. Westlake's blend of indoor and outdoor spaces is perfect for those Puget Sound rainy days that include some sun breaks." Thousands of people attended the grand opening, including Marie Dempcy, shown above.

**OPENING DAY.** "It was a big day when the door from the hotel to Westlake opened," recalls Marie Dempcy. Birney and Marie were invited to join the mayor and many others at the Seattle Center to ride the Monorail to Westlake Center for the first time. "There was a big ceremony at Westlake Center overlooking the new 'Park' with thousands of people and thousands of balloons. A lot of work was done around the hotel to prepare for this big event. The offices were taken out of the mezzanine to put in the new doors leading to Westlake. There was all new carpeting and furniture on that level, all new sidewalks all around the hotel, new plantings, and many other improvements. I never worked so hard . . . we all did . . . twelve hours a day, but it all came together the last day. It was the culmination of several years of working with the construction company as to the joining of the hotel and the project, the hallway and the hotel signage in Westlake. After all the festivities, when Birney and I returned to the hotel the staff surprised us with a champagne toast."

**METRO BUS TUNNEL CONSTRUCTION UNDER PINE STREET.** "There was a lot going on in our neighborhood in 1988. Just after our doors opened to Westlake in October, Pine Street opened on November 2, 1988, after 22 months of construction. It was such an important event, the city had a parade," recalls Marie Dempcy. As chair of the Northend Neighborhood Advisory Committee to Metro, Marie's role was to keep the line of communication open between shop owners along Pine Street while construction of the metro bus tunnel was under way. Access to those businesses needed to be maintained. Marie recalls, "Metro did what they could, but because the entire street was under construction, it was a dusty mess." (Left, courtesy of *Seattle Times*.)

*Certificate Of Appreciation*

This certificate is presented to

**Marie Dempcy**

in recognition of your service to the Pine Street community through the Northend Neighborhood Advisory Committee and in appreciation for the significant contribution you have made to Metro and the City of Seattle as a liaison to the Downtown Seattle Transit Project.

Alan J. Gibbs
Metro Executive Director

David Kalberer
Superintendent of the DSTP

George Benson
Seattle City Councilmember

*Municipality of Metropolitan Seattle*

✳ METRO

**MAYFLOWER PARK HOTEL LOBBY AND GUEST ROOM, 1992.** *Sunset* magazine described the Mayflower Park Hotel, "Small, with a personal touch . . . within walking distance of downtown. Boutique Hotel is a term used to define the indefinable—a small, individualistic establishment offering exceptional comfort, personalized service, and more than a little charm. It is the last ingredient that makes this classification risky, for charm is a matter of opinion. We have singled out nine Seattle hotels we think deserve this distinction. Mayflower Park Hotel has English country overtones, with antiques in the lobby and traditional furniture and floral comforters in the rooms. All the rooms in the 1927 hotel have been recently redecorated. The Mayflower connects to the four-level Westlake Center, a shopping mall with underground access to department stores."

**65TH ANNIVERSARY.** Jeannie Mar of *Seattle Times* reported, "When Birney Dempcy bought what is now the Mayflower Park Hotel, he never dreamed that he and his wife would actually run the place. Now eighteen years later, the profitable business is a way of life for the Dempcys. The hotel will celebrate its 65th anniversary this year. The Dempcys are collecting stories about the hotel's history. 'We are trying to reconstruct its true history,' Marie Dempcy said." (Courtesy of *Seattle Times*.)

**CHANGING CLIPPERS.** John Hinterberger of *Seattle Times* on April 4, 1996, reported, "The Mayflower Park Hotel has long had a great bar scene but Clippers dining room has lagged. Change is coming. Opening late this spring will be Andaluca, a Northwest-Mediterranean kitchen headed by Chef Don Curtiss with Kazzy and Associates doing the menus. Mesher-Shing designed the interiors." Hand-painted murals by local artists Robert Williamson and Irene Ingalls cover the walls. Jean Godden of *Seattle Times* reported on June 5, 1996, "Owners Birney and Marie Dempcy have focused on finding just the right look for Andaluca. The ceiling was painted dark olive, a shade picked to blend with the hand-painted walls and the Northwest Mediterranean cuisine."

ANDALUCA

Restaurant & Bar

407 Olive Way
Seattle, Washington 98101
206.382.6999

*Next to the Mayflower Park Hotel.
Open daily. Valet parking.*

**ANDALUCA.** Kerry Webster of *Seattle Times* reported on June 5, 1996, "The former Clippers Restaurant in the Mayflower Park Hotel reopens next week with a new name—Andaluca—and a Mediterranean theme. Mayflower Park Hotel owners Marie and Birney Dempcy are already calling it 'the jewel in the crown' of their vintage downtown hotel, which also boasts the well-regarded Oliver's. 'We are really excited about it. We felt that a really first-class restaurant would be the perfect last piece to finish our restoration of the hotel. The remodeled interior is casual, sophisticated, a little bit whimsical.' "

**JULIA CHILD WITH ANDALUCA CHEF DON CURTISS.** In October 1996, Julia Child visited Seattle to promote her latest book. She stopped by to see one of Seattle's newest restaurants and meet Executive Chef Don Curtiss.

HELPING SEATTLE FIREFIGHTERS. Andaluca Executive Chef Wayne Johnson (1999–2012) cooks up holiday meals for Seattle firefighters. Mayflower Park Hotel has a long tradition of being a good neighbor. The impact of September 11, 2001, touched everyone in the United States, and people across the country thanked those who serve in countless ways. Sherry Spring of *Seattle Times* reported, "Pioneer Square is a long way from the World Trade Center in New York City. But it's not so far from Fourth Avenue and Olive Way. That is where Wayne Johnson, Executive Chef at Andaluca toiled all day to make this portable feast of thanks. Like so many of us, Johnson's heart went out to the New York City firefighters and police officers who risked and lost their lives September 11, 2001. It reminded him of how much we in the Northwest also depend on our troops in blue." (Courtesy of *Seattle Times*.)

**SEAFAIR AT THE MAYFLOWER PARK HOTEL.** Over the past 20 years, to honor those of our Seattle Police Department who work during the annual Seafair Torchlight Parade, the Mayflower Park Hotel has hosted a deli dinner. This tradition has become something the Seattle Police Department looks forward to as a nice peaceful getaway in the midst of all the activity outside. The hotel feeds around 150 police officers, and they come by foot, bike, horse, and car. The Mayflower Park Hotel was recognized formally when the hotel received a Citizen Appreciation Award to acknowledge this deli dinner. Accepting certificates below are, from left to right, Marie Dempcy, owner; Sarah Lorenzen, executive chef; and Steve Johansson, beverage manager.

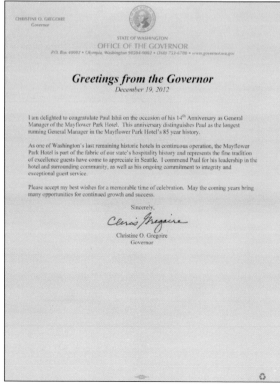

### Greetings from the Governor
*December 19, 2012*

I am delighted to congratulate Paul Ishii on the occasion of his 14th Anniversary as General Manager of the Mayflower Park Hotel. This anniversary distinguishes Paul as the longest running General Manager in the Mayflower Park Hotel's 85 year history.

As one of Washington's last remaining historic hotels in continuous operation, the Mayflower Park Hotel is part of the fabric of our state's hospitality history and represents the fine tradition of excellence guests have come to appreciate in Seattle. I commend Paul for his leadership in the hotel and surrounding community, as well as his ongoing commitment to integrity and exceptional guest service.

Please accept my best wishes for a memorable time of celebration. May the coming years bring many opportunities for continued growth and success.

Sincerely,

Christine O. Gregoire
Governor

**PAUL ISHII.** In 1998, Paul Ishii was named general manager of the Mayflower Park Hotel. In 2012, he became the longest-tenured general manager at the hotel since 1927 and received acknowledgment from Gov. Christine Gregoire. His accomplishments include gaining the hotel membership in Historic Hotels of America. In addition, he has served as president of the Washington Lodging Association, Seattle Hotel Association, and Seattle Rotary; founding board member of Seattle Tourism Authority; founding member of 4Culture; and board member of Higher Education Coordinating Board of Washington State. He was also named Silver Plume General Manager of the Year. Ishii says, "What has kept me here at the Mayflower all these years? The people. I have been lucky to work with a staff dedicated to delivering a level of service that goes above and beyond."

**CHRISTMASTIME.** Christmas at the Mayflower Park Hotel has become a holiday tradition since 1974. A December 5, 1974, log entry states, "Looking like Christmas at the Mayflower." Thus began a hands-on tradition of Marie Dempcy, who personally oversaw the installation of Christmas trees in the lobby and in Oliver's. "The hotel is our favorite place to stay in Seattle, and it looked lovely with all the holiday decorations," said a Mayflower Park Hotel guest. The bannisters pictured here are an original feature of the hotel.

**CHRISTMAS TREE IN OLIVER'S.** One guest recalled, "We just returned from our annual Seattle downtown trip and our stay at the Mayflower Park Hotel. It was a wonderful weekend. I see the same faces every year, which tells me this must be an amazing place to work if people never leave. From the Front Desk to the Servers in Oliver's to the Bell Captains and Valet Staff to the Housekeeping—fabulous people! Thank you for making our holiday weekend so special!" Another patron said, "Many thanks for another memorable holiday at the Mayflower. Our grandson loved looking out the windows watching traffic and the trains in the Macy's window. Have a happy holiday season. See you next year!"

CHRISTMAS TRADITIONS. "I am so glad I chose your hotel to begin a Christmas tradition with my granddaughter," said a guest. "It is a special honor to stay at the Mayflower each December for one night as we do our holiday shopping, have Santa photos taken at Macy's, then meet my son and his wife for dinner. Each year we play the guessing game of what floor we will be assigned and what type of a view of the city we will have. What a delight we have in putting on our special hotel robes and reading the story about Eloise, a little girl who lived in a hotel. Every staff member is always friendly and helpful with fun conversation and well-being about their working environment. Thank you for making our stay so special and we look forward to many years ahead at the Mayflower."

**INVITATIONS TO THE ART OF HOSPITALITY.** In creative collaboration, the Mayor's Office of Arts and Cultural Affairs, 4Culture, the Fifth Avenue Theatre, and Seattle's Convention and Visitors Bureau have become presenters of the Art of Hospitality Gallery and Reception. "The Art of Hospitality is an exhibit to promote creativity and recognition for the employees of Seattle's boutique hotels," said Paul Ishii, general manager of the Mayflower Park Hotel, the originator of the event. "It shows and communicates the other side of talented people who work in the hospitality industry in our city and gives the community a chance to see how versatile and well-rounded our employees are." The Art of Hospitality showcases many forms of artistic talent, including oil, watercolor, and mixed-media paintings; photography; sculptures; culinary art; handiwork; and interactive art, such as theatrical work and music. Over the years, the beneficiary of a percentage of the proceeds went to Seattle Academy of Fine Art, Haas Foundation, and John Muir Elementary School Arts. The invitation at left was designed by Patrick, who has been an Oliver's bartender for over 10 years.

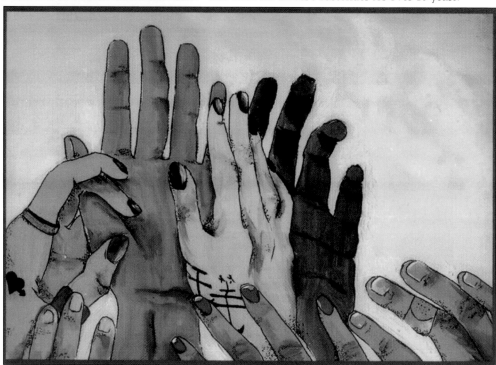

**CHEF WAYNE JOHNSON.** Chef Wayne Johnson of Andaluca Restaurant (1999–2012) appeared on the Food Network show *Iron Chef America* on July 31, 2011. Chef Johnson challenged Iron Chef Michael Symon. Glenn Drosendahl of *Puget Sound Business Journal* reported, "Cucumber? Really. That was the secret ingredient Wayne Johnson, Executive Chef at Seattle's Andaluca Restaurant, had to work with on Food Network's Iron Chef America. Considering that he had to create five courses in an hour using that ingredient, you might think the word ran through him like a cold dagger. But no, 'I was kind of excited,' Johnson said, 'because we had worked a little with cucumbers. So I was like, we can do this. Alas, as underdog to Symon, the designated Iron Chef, Johnson did not win . . . at least not on the show. But his food—created with the help of Andaluca Sous Chef Dawn Kale and Nami Soto—looked great, made for a close competition and created some buzz for Andaluca."

# Iron Chef America

## Wayne Johnson
## versus
## Michael Symon

### Sunday, July 31st at 10pm ET/PT

Watch Chef Wayne Johnson on

Food Network Channel challenging

Chef Michael Symon on

Sunday, July 31st at 10pm ET/PT,

Monday August 1st at 1am ET/PT and

Thursday, August 4th at 11pm ET/PT.

Tune in to find out if Seattle's Chef

Wayne Johnson can beat the tough

Michael Symon from Chicago.

Facebook.com/andaluca

Twitter.com/andaluca

**WONDERFUL EMPLOYEES AND GREAT ROOMS.** The following Mayflower memory was submitted by a devoted sister, "Our family was raised in Seattle starting in 1945 and has many memories of Seafair parades. Our sister is enjoying her final months of her life and wanted to watch the Seafair Torchlight Parade one more time in person. Her physical limitations made viewing the parade on the street out of the realm of possibilities. We turned to your hotel as a solution. Your staff—especially the Reservations staff—were very helpful and patient with me as I continually called to be reassured that this 'bucket list' idea would be a night for my sister's family to remember forever. I spoke to my sister while she watched the parade from her hotel room. She was having a fantastic time. Life is good. We hope you realize that you have wonderful employees. Thank you to all your staff for their efforts to make the night of July 28, 2012, a memorable one."

**WEDDINGS!** The elegantly appointed Fireside Room is located on the mezzanine level of the hotel. Once known as the Ladies' Lounge, this location has a long history of unforgettable ceremonies and wedding receptions. "I simply cannot say enough good things about our wedding at the Mayflower Park Hotel," said a present-day bride. "The service was exquisite, from our first meeting until our last guests from the East Coast checked out with smiles on their faces. We are a traditional couple that do not go for the über-mod, trendy kind of thing, and the Mayflower Park whispered 'classic elegance' when everywhere else we looked seemed to be yelling about mason jar cocktails and food truck catering. The Mayflower is just a beautiful hotel—it is unlike any other in Seattle." Says another bride, "The historic feel is apparent the moment you walk in to the lobby, the atmosphere is very elegant." (Above, courtesy of Bev Hawes [bride]; right, courtesy of Sara Brooke [bride] Photography.)

ANTIQUES AT THE MAYFLOWER PARK HOTEL. The beautiful c. 1780 clock at left is an English Chippendale mahogany long-case clock by William Taylor of Whitehaven, purchased in May 1988 from a downtown Seattle antique store. Below the gilded French chateau mirror sits the c. 1820 French Empire chest with black marble top. Beautiful floral arrangements placed on the chest, the center table of the lobby, and at the front desk, have become a Mayflower Park Hotel tradition.

MAYFLOWER PARK HOTEL PROMOTIONAL PIECE. This promotional piece is a key component in marketing the hotel. A strong partner and supporter of the arts, the hotel collaborates with a variety of packages when there is a major exhibit at the Seattle Art Museum or a special theater performance in town. This ad would be found in performance programs. Since 1927, a consistent feature promoted about the hotel is that it is "Seattle's Premier Location."

**MAYFLOWER PARK HOTEL POSTCARD.** Drew Burnham, a well-known Canadian artist, was commissioned to do an original watercolor of the hotel's exterior. It was almost a year-long project making sure that the picture was perfect, sending it back and forth from Canada to Seattle. This is the official picture the hotel uses on note cards and promotional pieces as well as Christmas cards. Watercolor postcards of hotels are not common anymore, but they were years ago, as evidenced by the Mayflower Park Hotel's historical postcard collection. The Bergonian Hotel had a watercolor painting depicted on a postcard, as seen on page 15. The Hotel Mayflower had a watercolor painting depicted on a postcard, as seen on page 39. All use the Fourth and Olive view of the hotel.

**ANOTHER BANNER YEAR.** Each year, these banners are replaced to commemorate the Mayflower Park Hotel's distinction of being the longest continuously operating hotel in Seattle. (Courtesy of Michael B Photography.)

**AN ENTRANCE TO HOSPITALITY.** Pictured is Michael B with his signature bowler hat extending a warm welcome to all incoming guests. He has been with the hotel for over 17 years and will tell guests that it is true—history does repeat itself—as the image on page 8 so clearly reflects. This sentiment is beautifully articulated by early food writer Jean Anthelme Brillat-Savarin, "To invite a person into your house is to take charge of his happiness for as long as he is under your roof." Repeat guests Jack and Clara Frost agree, "You are really our 'extended family' and it is always a delight to walk through those front doors to smiles and hugs."

# *Four*

# COCKTAILS AT THE MAYFLOWER
## 1949 TO PRESENT

Enjoying a cocktail at the Mayflower has been a Seattle tradition since 1949.

Washington State legalized cocktail lounges in 1948, and the Hotel Mayflower became Seattle's first hotel to open a cocktail lounge. The Carousel Room, a small, cozy bar, had a total capacity of 19. This tiny cocktail lounge was so successful that it was expanded in 1951. Merry-go-round horses, suspended from the ceiling, galloped overhead. Clowns and the carnival spirit were reflected everywhere. The room now had a total capacity of 75, and the menu featured items such as the "Paul Bunyan Hamburger" and cocktails like the "Carnival Cooler." The windows that once showcased the items for sale in Bartell Drugs were replaced with outer walls of blue and a big colorful clown holding illuminated balloons. This is what young, newlywed Marie Dempcy saw on a cold winter day as she tried to get warm in the Bon Marche across the street. She was looking for a job to support her husband, Birney, through the University of Washington Law School. The Carousel Room was a very popular place to go, one which the Dempcys could not afford at the time. Longingly, she looked at the Carousel Room from across the street, hoping one day she could afford to eat there.

In 1976, Oliver's replaced the Carousel Room and became the state of Washington's first daylight bar. Until then, Washington blue laws prohibited anyone from looking into a lounge where hard liquor was sold. With new laws customers could now look out on the street scene. Through floor-to-ceiling windowpanes pedestrians could watch the bartender mixing drinks. The marble for the tabletops in Oliver's was salvaged from the lobby of the historic White-Henry-Stuart Building. The 15-foot ceiling incorporated a crystal chandelier purchased from Italy. The remodel of Oliver's and its subsequent success were the deciding factors for the Dempcys to continue to invest in the rest of the hotel. In capturing the historic architecture and enduring charm, it set the tone for how the rest of the hotel would be remodeled.

MINUTES OF MEETING OF BOARD OF DIRECTORS

HOTEL MAYFLOWER CO.

December 8, 1948

Pursuant to notice and waiver of notice, a meeting of the Board of Directors of Hotel Mayflower Co. was held December 8, 1948, at the Mayflower Hotel in Seattle, Washington, a quorum being present and all directors concurring in the business transacted at the meeting.

Financial reports were presented and business policies discussed. It was stated that application would be made for an "H" license under the Washington State Liquor Act, as amended by Initiative 171, and that plans were being drawn and estimates secured on cost of installation of a cocktail bar. It was stated that this would require substantial outlay of capital, the present estimate of officers being approximately $ 7,000.

The President stated, however, that earnings were sufficient and cash available with which to pay a dividend of $2.00 per share. Upon motion duly made, seconded and carried, the following resolution was adopted:

    BE IT RESOLVED: That a dividend of $2.00 per share upon the outstanding stock of this company is hereby declared, said dividend to be paid December 15, 1948, to shareholders of record December 10, 1948.

There being no further business, the meeting adjourned.

_____ President

_____ Secretary

A COCKTAIL LOUNGE. The December 8, 1948, Hotel Mayflower meeting minutes show that plans were put into motion to open a cocktail lounge. "There had been, at one time, a soda fountain in that location. Later it was a storage room. This was cleaned out, when public bars were allowed by the state," said a past hotel employee. Mayflower historians believe the transition from a Bartell Drugs soda fountain to cocktail lounge was expedited because the physical bar was already in place, resulting in the Carousel being the first hotel cocktail lounge in Seattle. (See page 45 for the 1946 bill of sale.) *Front!* magazine reported in July 1949, "Last fall Washington legalized cocktail lounges and the real rush was on. By July 1949, Western Hotels Incorporated had sixteen cocktail lounges. The management of the Mayflower forsook history and chose the name 'Carousel Room' for its cocktail lounge. Little merry-go-rounds will form the decorative motif. It will be a small, cozy lounge." (Courtesy of Manuscripts, Archives, and Special Collections, Washington State University Libraries.)

**THE CAROUSEL ROOM.** The Carousel Room at the Hotel Mayflower was an immediate success. The April 18, 1949, Hotel Mayflower meeting minutes report, "The Chairman then stated that under the new law authorizing the sale of liquor by the drink, this company had had a cocktail lounge in operation for six days and that from all indications it was thought that this division of the company would show a continuous small profit." *Front!* magazine reported in July 1949, "Of the twelve Western Hotels in Washington, nine are planning lounges. The Benjamin Franklin will open the Outrigger, the Roosevelt will open the Rough Rider Room, the Cascadian in Wenatchee will open the Cascadian's Lounge, the Marcus Whitman in Walla Walla will open the Wishing Well, the Winthrop in Tacoma will open the Saber Room. The New Washington in Seattle, the Governor in Olympia, and the Leopold in Bellingham have not decided on names." (Courtesy of Manuscripts, Archives, and Special Collections, Washington State University Libraries.)

**CAROUSEL ROOM AT THE HOTEL MAYFLOWER.** *Pacific Northwest* in April 1952 reported, "Many unusual construction features make the room particularly interesting. Real merry-go-round horses, suspended from the ceiling, gallop overhead. Specially made tables were cast with six different kinds of terrazzo with a clown's head in the center composed of different colors of terrazzo and outlined in brass. The room has the most compact and complete charcoal broiler and kitchen in Seattle, all fully open to the public's inspection. Most fascinating of the conversation pieces in the room are the intricate Lucite carousels that rest on a ledge to adjoin the booths. Approximately eighteen inches high, they are indirectly illuminated by lights that constantly and slowly change colors. For all its attractions, the Carousel is a quiet, restful place." (Courtesy of the Clodfelter family.)

**CAROUSEL STAFF IN LIVELY UNIFORMS.** *Front!* magazine reported in January 1952, "The carnival touch at the Mayflower's new Carousel Room is carried out in the lively uniforms worn by the waitresses." Ready to welcome customers above, are, from left to right, Mary Lou Kilkenny, Lois Allen, Retha Kird, Dawn Palmer, and Helen Culbertson. Other staff members in the room pictured below are, from left to right, (front row), Bill Strong, assistant bar manager; Jack Borg, manager; and Clem Summerfield and Ray Barnes, chefs; (second row), Skee Gardner and Fred McKenzie, bartenders. (Both, courtesy of Manuscripts, Archives, and Special Collections, Washington State University Libraries.)

**FRONT AND BACK OF CAROUSEL MENU.** The back of the menu describes the Carousel theme, "Among our fondest recollections are those of the lovely, leaping, tuneful merry-go-round, so when we planned this room we named it the Carousel, which is the French name for this whirling carnival attraction. The carousels were first popularized in France as a feature attraction in the small carnivals that played so important a part in the 17th- and 18th-century social life. To the hamlets of that day they brought romance and adventure. . . . With the world so intent on getting somewhere it is relaxing to just whirl musically around and around and get nowhere at all. Though our Carousel does not whirl we want to express the same carnival spirit and provide many charming moments for your enjoyment." (Both, courtesy of Heather McColm.)

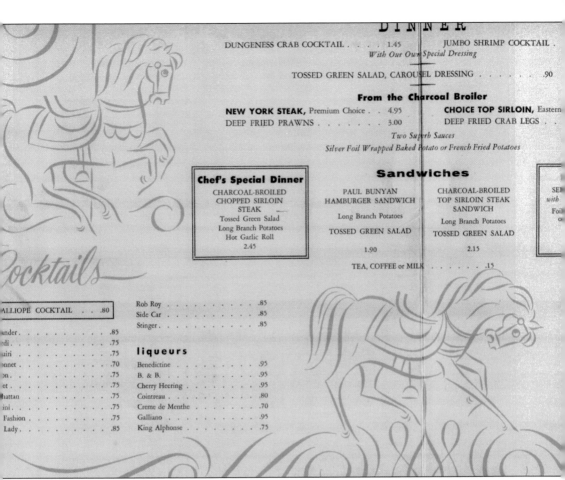

## DINNER

DUNGENESS CRAB COCKTAIL . . . . . 1.45     JUMBO SHRIMP COCKTAIL .

*With Our Own Special Dressing*

TOSSED GREEN SALAD, CAROUSEL DRESSING . . . . . . . .90

### From the Charcoal Broiler

**NEW YORK STEAK,** Premium Choice . . 4.95     **CHOICE TOP SIRLOIN,** Eastern

DEEP FRIED PRAWNS . . . . . . . 3.00     DEEP FRIED CRAB LEGS . .

*Two Superb Sauces*

*Silver Foil Wrapped Baked Potato or French Fried Potatoes*

**Chef's Special Dinner**

CHARCOAL-BROILED
CHOPPED SIRLOIN
STEAK —
Tossed Green Salad
Long Branch Potatoes
Hot Garlic Roll
2.45

### Sandwiches

| PAUL BUNYAN HAMBURGER SANDWICH | CHARCOAL-BROILED TOP SIRLOIN STEAK SANDWICH | SE with Foil o |
|---|---|---|
| Long Branch Potatoes | Long Branch Potatoes | |
| TOSSED GREEN SALAD | TOSSED GREEN SALAD | |
| 1.90 | 2.15 | |

TEA, COFFEE or MILK . . . . . . .15

*Cocktails*

| ALLIOPE COCKTAIL . . .80 | | Rob Roy . . . . . . . . . . . . .85 |
|---|---|---|
| ander . . . . . . . . . . . . .85 | | Side Car . . . . . . . . . . . .85 |
| edi . . . . . . . . . . . . . . .75 | | Stinger . . . . . . . . . . . . .85 |
| uiri . . . . . . . . . . . . . .75 | | |
| onnet . . . . . . . . . . . . .70 | **liqueurs** | |
| on . . . . . . . . . . . . . . .75 | Benedictine . . . . . . . . . .95 | |
| et . . . . . . . . . . . . . . .75 | B. & B. . . . . . . . . . . . . .95 | |
| hattan . . . . . . . . . . . .75 | Cherry Heering . . . . . . . .95 | |
| ini . . . . . . . . . . . . . . .75 | Cointreau . . . . . . . . . . .80 | |
| Fashion . . . . . . . . . . . .75 | Creme de Menthe . . . . . .70 | |
| Lady . . . . . . . . . . . . . .85 | Galliano . . . . . . . . . . . .95 | |
| | King Alphonse . . . . . . . .75 | |

**CAROUSEL MENU.** The menu features gargantuan charcoal-broiled hot dogs and Paul Bunyan hamburgers. Among the cocktails are a Carnival Cooler and a Pink Lady. "In 1951, my three friends and I, all underage, decided to have our first cocktail in the Carousel Room," said one guest. "We decided we would order a Pink Lady. We were properly dressed, and I specifically remember wearing a blue suit, blue shoes with blue purse, white shift, white gloves and white hat. We came after work, around 6pm, which in 1951 was a respectable time for ladies to be out. The Server probably knew we were underage, but because we looked so respectable, served us anyway. As the Server took our order, one of my friends ordered milk . . . to the shock of the rest of us. She got her milk, but then ordered her Pink Lady." (Courtesy of Heather McColm.)

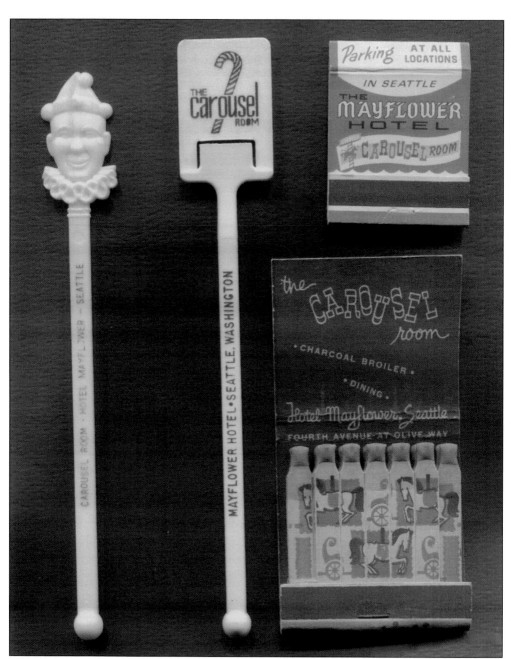

**CAROUSEL MATCHBOOK AND CAROUSEL ROOM COCKTAIL STIR STICKS AT THE MAYFLOWER HOTEL.**
The Carousel matchbooks creatively display the lively and colorful aspects of the cocktail lounge. The outside of the matchbook is blue with red and white showing playful carnival graphics. The graphics communicate that the restaurant is a fun place to be. Open the matchbook, and the lively theme continues with images on the matches. The Carousel stir sticks complement the restaurant and add to the visual adventure consistent with the carnival atmosphere. Stir sticks with the clown were white, red, blue, green, and yellow. Stir sticks with the candy canes were white with red graphics, which matched the door handles to the Carousel Room. Cocktails offered included a Calliope Cocktail and a Carnival Cooler. (Courtesy of Steve Vlah and Craig Packer.)

EXTERIOR VIEW OF THE CAROUSEL ROOM AT THE HOTEL MAYFLOWER, 1952. *Pacific Northwest* in April 1952 reported, "The Carousel is conveniently located for downtown Seattle shoppers. Its main entrance is directly across the street from the Bon Marche, one of Seattle's largest department stores, and only a few blocks from the other large stores and theaters. The exterior design was worked out to make the most of this location. Done in bright red, white and blue colored Vitrolite, it is dominated by a huge clown holding illuminated plastic balloons. Its location makes the Carousel popular for luncheons." This is what Marie Dempcy saw in 1955. Little did she know that, 20 years later, she would own the Carousel Room, close it due to its bad reputation, and embark on a legacy known as Oliver's. (Courtesy of Museum of History & Industry.)

**CAROUSEL ROOM BOARDED UP, 1974.** When the Dempcys purchased the Mayflower Hotel, the lounge, restaurant, and banquet rooms were leased out. Becoming more involved with the operations of the hotel, they found that troubling front desk log entries, such as "Marlena S. in room 615 is really Marlena W. She tries to set up business here for herself and her pimp," were common. Birney Dempcy decided to come to the hotel and see what was going on in the evenings. He sat on the steps leading to the mezzanine and waited. Soon, the pay telephones across from the elevators and outside the entrance to the Carousel Room would ring. A lady would come out of the Carousel, answer the phone, and then take the elevator to an unknown floor. After watching this occur over and over, the decision was easy. Buy out the lease and close the Carousel Room! *Seattle Weekly* reported, "The Carousel Room was ripped out and replaced by false fronts promising a new restaurant."

**Windows Revealed.** Polly Lane at the *Seattle Times* reported on May 8, 1974, "Revitalization is planned of the ground-floor restaurant (formerly operated as the Carousel Room)." Architects were contacted, concepts presented, and Robert Mesher of Kumata & Mesher was selected to design the new bar. His design included taking the architectural elements of the era in which the hotel was built and return classic design to the room. A key element of that design was to remove the outside walls and install windows that were in place when the hotel opened in 1927. After a year of false fronts, the plywood was removed, and in its place were floor-to-ceiling windows showcasing street-side activity. "It was a big day," the Dempcys reflected.

**WHAT TO NAME THE NEW BAR?** During the construction process in early 1976, Birney and Marie were having a terrible time coming up with a name for the new bar. One evening, the Dempcys were at a dinner party and the topic came up. One of their friends, Ann Wright, said, "Well, it's on Fourth and Olive . . . how about Oliver's?" Birney and Marie loved the name. The idea came months prior to the opening of the new bar. During that time, they also were updating the hotel restaurant on the other side of the lobby. For a very short time, they decided to call the restaurant Oliver's. They even painted "Oliver's" on the window outside. Two weeks later, the paint was scraped off, and Oliver's became the name of the new bar.

# Mayflower Park Hotel

coffee shop, lounge and convention room

| | |
|---|---|
| **LOCATION:** | 405 Olive Way<br>Seattle, Washington |
| **OWNER:** | Westlake Park Associates<br>Birney Dempcy, Principal<br>682-1505 |
| **ARCHITECT:** | Kumata and Mesher AIA<br>Gerald Kumata 282-9271<br>Robert Mesher 622-4981 |
| **ENGINEERING:** | Mechanical: West Seattle Furnace<br>Electrical: Ron Gracey |
| **SCOPE OF PROJECT:** | Convert existing spaces with new finishes,<br>mechanical and electrical systems,<br>casework and equipment.<br><br>4,600 s.f. Finished Floor Area<br><br>Cost per s.f. $45.00 (1976) |

OLIVER'S OPENING. Oliver's opened on June 26, 1976, as the state of Washington's first daylight bar. Until then, Washington blue laws prohibited anyone from looking into a bar where hard liquor was sold. *Seattle Weekly* on August 4, 1976, reported, "By a fortuitous coincidence, plans for the bar were being drawn up by the designers, Kumata and Mesher, just as a regulation prohibiting minors from viewing preparation of mixed drinks was being removed by the State Liquor Board. This is a landmark change of liquor regulations, since until now it has been effectively impossible to have a cocktail lounge that could be viewed from the street. Now the effect is dramatically opposite at the corner of Fourth and Olive, where the bar is illuminated by 10 floor-to-ceiling windows, each with 25 panes of glass. The room is flooded with natural light, classical piano music carefully chosen . . . and the mood is urbane and convivial. The busy street scene outside is framed by the classic architecture of the Bon Marche and the Securities and Times Square Buildings."

**OLIVER'S LOUNGE.** *Seattle Times* reported on June 27, 1976, "The 1,400 square foot bar will seat eighty-five. Marble from the White-Henry-Stuart Building was used for the tabletops in the New York–San Francisco–style lounge." In 1976, Birney Dempcy's law practice was in the IBM Building on Seneca Street. Each day during the construction phase of Oliver's, he would walk down during lunch to inspect the progress. Walking past the historic 1910 White-Henry-Stuart Building being torn down to build Rainier Square, he noticed the salvage crew removing marble walls from the lobby. He asked if they would sell the marble. A price was agreed upon, and the salvage company delivered the marble walls to a cutter to have them made into tabletops for the new lounge. Those tabletops remain in Oliver's today, a part of Seattle history.

**WITH A STREET VIEW.** "The unexpected sight of watching a bartender from the street, wipe a glass and measure a shot of Jim Beam is both startling and pleasurable," reported the *Seattle Weekly* on August 4, 1976. "I worked at Oliver's in the early years. As the first daylight bar in the area we really drew a crowd," said a past employee. The original design of Oliver's placed the bar in the lower section of the room. The design wasn't working until it was suggested to put the bar in front of the window, which turned out to be Oliver's signature feature. (Courtesy of the *Seattle Weekly*.)

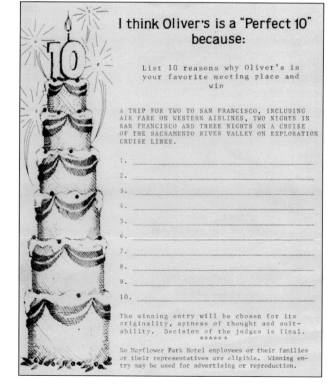

**I think Oliver's is a "Perfect 10" because:**

List 10 reasons why Oliver's is your favorite meeting place and win

A TRIP FOR TWO TO SAN FRANCISCO, INCLUDING AIR FARE ON WESTERN AIRLINES, TWO NIGHTS IN SAN FRANCISCO AND THREE NIGHTS ON A CRUISE OF THE SACRAMENTO RIVER VALLEY ON EXPLORATION CRUISE LINES.

1. _____
2. _____
3. _____
4. _____
5. _____
6. _____
7. _____
8. _____
9. _____
10. _____

The winning entry will be chosen for its originality, aptness of thought and suitability. Decision of the judges is final.
\*\*\*\*\*\*
No Mayflower Park Hotel employees or their families or their representatives are eligible. Winning entry may be used for advertising or reproduction.

**OLIVER'S 10TH BIRTHDAY, JUNE 1986.** Oliver's had a big birthday party and contest for patrons to list 10 reasons why Oliver's was their favorite downtown bar. *Seattle Guide* reported, "A fun extra on Friday night, the 27th, will be authentic Dixieland music by the very popular Uptown Lowdown Jazz Band, starting at 6 p.m."

**OLIVER'S MARTINI CLASSIC CHALLENGE.** Who makes Seattle's best martini? The genius behind the idea was Marc Nowak, the Mayflower Park Hotel general manager from 1990 to 1998. "What began as an innocent challenge by Oliver's to Vons for Seattle's best martini has now blossomed into a full-scale event! After Vons declined, we invited the Metropolitan Grill, Il Bistro and the Four Seasons Garden Court to join in the Challenge and now have a stylish progressive tasting which will 'sip out' the Best Martini," stated an internal Mayflower memo dated September 25, 1992. Sherry Grindeland from the *Journal American* reported, "We went from the Mayflower to Il Bistro at Pike Place Market to the Garden Court at the Four Seasons Olympic to the Metropolitan Grill."

**First-annual Martini Classic Bartenders.** "Where do you go for the best martini in town? That was the challenge Friday night when seven judges set out to judge martinis at four of the city's classiest lounges. Obviously, judging the 'first martini classic' was a hardship assignment. But, when asked to participate, I hesitated only long enough to ensure I wouldn't have to drive," reported Jean Godden, *Seattle Times* staff columnist, on October 12, 1992. The first-annual Martini Classic bartenders pictured here are, from left to right, Michael Vezzoni, Four Seasons; Murray Stenson, Il Bistro; JoJo Beaulieu, Metropolitan Grill; and Mike Rule, Oliver's. The judges included Jean Godden, John Hinterberger, Richard Kinssies, John Koerper, Lori McKean, Sherry Grindeland, Dick Foley, and Mike Siegel. Sherry Grindeland from the *Journal American* reported, "Mike Rule, Bartender at Oliver's at the Mayflower Park Hotel, has come up with a good idea for the second annual taste. He's going to have a Bloody Mary contest next morning."

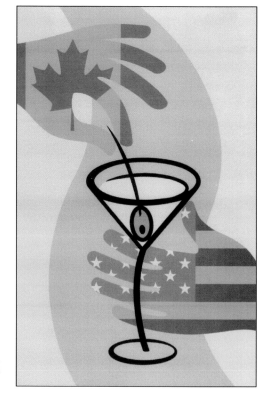

**SIXTH-ANNUAL SEATTLE MARTINI CLASSIC CHALLENGE INVITATION.** Jean Godden of *Seattle Times* reported on February 9, 1998, "Limos ferried the arbiters to four worthy contenders. The eight judges agonized, but finally gave the nod to an expertly concocted cocktail mixed by bartender Mike Rule at Oliver's, the defending champ."

**FIRST-ANNUAL INTERNATIONAL MARTINI CHALLENGE INVITATION.** Cynthia Nims reported in the July–August 1999 issue of *Cheers* magazine, "Seattle's Mayflower Park Hotel has turned a one-shot Martini promo into a widely-anticipated international event." Oliver's won the Seattle Classic Martini Award, and Gerard Lounge won the Vancouver, British Columbia, Classic Martini Award. Both invitations were created by John Dempcy, son of the Dempcys.

**LOCAL SEATTLE CELEBRITY JUDGES AT MARTINI CLASSIC.** Jean Godden, then writer for the *Seattle Times* and now member of the Seattle City Council, is seen above with John Hinterberger, then food critic for *Seattle Times*. Gary Crow, then of 103.7 KMTT-FM and now of 102.5 KZOK and the long-standing telephone voice of the Mayflower Park Hotel for all calls placed on hold, is pictured at right. Oliver's won the Martini Classic challenge in 1993, 1994, 1995, 1996, and 1998 and the International Challenge in 1999 and 2000, which was the last competition. The Mayflower Park Hotel gratefully acknowledges the participation of all judges, contenders, contributors, and spectators who made this a truly celebrated downtown Seattle tradition.

**THE CHRISTMAS SPIRIT.** In 1996, Santa was sighted at the hotel. In the 1980s and 1990s, the hotel had two very special guests at Christmas, the Westlake Santa Claus and the Bon Marche Santa Claus. It took special coordination to make sure that when the Westlake Santa was in our lobby, the Bon Marche Santa was not. It was important not to confuse the children! Great Figgy Pudding Street Carolers also visited the hotel. For over 25 years, this team has made Oliver's its first stop, enjoying a beverage and sharing its first carol. Then they announce their departure and lead their loyal fans to the streets of Seattle to participate in the Great Figgy Pudding Street Corner Caroling Competition.

**OLIVER'S, A SEATTLE LANDMARK.** Tan Vinh, a *Seattle Times* staff writer, reported on June 22, 2011, "Thirty-five years is an eternity in the bar racket, so Oliver's has plenty of stories to tell and people to thank. When Oliver's opened on June 26, 1976, it was one of the most controversial bar debuts in Seattle. The state had just lifted an esoteric law that banned cocktail lounges from having windows. Harvey Wallbangers and Tequila Sunrises were the 'in' drinks then. These days, Oliver's, one of the region's longest operating hotel bars, is known for martinis." To our loyal family of guests, thank you. It is your affinity for elegance and reverence for generous service that has made cocktails at the Mayflower a Seattle tradition.

# DISCOVER THOUSANDS OF LOCAL HISTORY BOOKS
## FEATURING MILLIONS OF VINTAGE IMAGES

Arcadia Publishing, the leading local history publisher in the United States, is committed to making history accessible and meaningful through publishing books that celebrate and preserve the heritage of America's people and places.

Find more books like this at
**www.arcadiapublishing.com**

Search for your hometown history, your old
stomping grounds, and even your favorite sports team.